D1825847

Can We Read Letters?

Can We Read Letters?

Reflections on Fundamental Issues in Reading and Dyslexia Research

Finn Egil Tønnessen

with Per Henning Uppstad
National Centre for Reading Education and Research,
Stavanger, Norway

SENSE PUBLISHERS
ROTTERDAM / BOSTON / TAIPEI

A C.I.P. record for this book is available from the Library of Congress.

ISBN 978-94-6209-954-8 (paperback)
ISBN 978-94-6209-955-5 (hardback)
ISBN 978-94-6209-956-2 (e-book)

Published by: Sense Publishers,
P.O. Box 21858, 3001 AW Rotterdam, The Netherlands
https://www.sensepublishers.com/

Printed on acid-free paper

ADVANCE PRAISE

Can We Read Letters? provides a scholarly, yet approachable, treatise, provoking the reader to reconsider both current and historical accounts of reading development and of the impairment we call 'dyslexia'. – *Professor Joel B. Talcott, Aston University, Editor of Dyslexia*

In their new book, Finn Egil Tønnessen and Per Henning Uppstad provide a set of theoretical and philosophical reflections on research in reading and dyslexia. It is a pleasure to welcome this book, which reflects the many contributions made by researchers at the National Centre for Reading Education and Research in Stavanger, Norway. – *Professor Usha Goswami, University of Cambridge*

This is a scholarly and challenging work which raises a number of issues for current reading research in relation to the philosophy of science. – *Professor Angela Fawcett, University of Sheffield, UK, Former Editor of Dyslexia*

TABLE OF CONTENTS

PREFACE

Internationally there has been a major increase in activity within reading and dyslexia research over the past three or four decades. This is a reasonable development given that the importance of having good reading skills has grown ever greater in our modern society, where information and education take pride of place. However, that increase in research activity has not resulted in more attention being devoted to the fundamental questions within the field. Most branches of science, once they attain a certain level in their development, tend to ask more and more questions pertaining to the philosophy of science. This is crucial for assessing the quality of research and for deciding the way forward. Empirical researchers may well find such theoretical issues rather alien to their work, but there is in fact a great deal of practical benefit to be drawn from careful consideration of them. It is hard to imagine a Nobel laureate who has never reflected upon issues relating to the philosophy of science.

When I first embarked upon research into reading and dyslexia twenty-five years ago, I was uncertain where to concentrate my efforts within a field which was becoming more and more multifaceted. The deciding factor turned out to be my background – and interest – in medicine, psychology, logic and the philosophy of science. My PhD thesis focused on the hypotheses and findings published shortly before by Norman Geschwind and Albert Galaburda about the relationship between brain lateralisation (left-handedness), immunological diseases and dyslexia. I remain fascinated to this day by the creativity and boldness of those hypotheses, but that did not prevent me from presenting questions and critical objections in my thesis. In my opinion, one characteristic of good research is precisely that it inspires new hypotheses and new studies.

However, describing and explaining reading and dyslexia on the basis of neurology alone did not seem enough to me, and nor did I think the answers provided by behaviourism were sufficient. This is why I enthusiastically launched into studies based on cognitive psychology. As time went on, though, that school of thought also came to feel too one-sided and too limited. I found connectionism to be a good way of unifying these different approaches, but after a while I instead started to search for the solution in the concept of 'skill', which I considered capable of bringing all of these different schools of thought together. In my opinion, it is fairly obvious that reading is above all a 'skill' or 'procedural knowledge'. It represents primarily implicit – not explicit – knowledge. For my definition of 'skill', I borrowed the concept of 'automaticity' from behaviourism and that of 'awareness' from cognitive psychology, but it was clear to me that they could not be unified through simple addition or combination, so I turned to philosophy for a solution.

I found it in Aristotle's ideas about theoretical and practical activity. These were ideas that I had studied in the 1980s, and I quickly realised that the word 'skill' was a good fit. In modern terminology, this word is often associated with the performance of technical or mechanical tasks in an automatic, flawless manner. However, what I translate as 'skill' in the context of reading is something that Aristotle considers to be a consequence of humans having both physical qualities and mental or spiritual ones. Through training, people develop skills that bring together automaticity and awareness (compare the concept of 'embodied knowledge' used by phenomenologists and others). One obvious example of such a skill is swimming. From a historical point of view, reading is nothing but a more recent example.

But what does this mean when it comes to explaining the causes of dyslexia? In my opinion, Rod Nicolson and Angela Fawcett launched an interesting hypothesis by claiming that dyslexics have problems with automatisation that can be traced back to abnormal conditions in the cerebellum. What is more, that hypothesis seems to be supported by empirical studies. However, I think they place too little weight on awareness. John Stein has contributed a perhaps even more fruitful hypothesis which is based on the distinction between the magnocellular and parvocellular systems. This hypothesis was originally linked to the visual system but has since been expanded to encompass the auditory system and sensory activity in general. As I understand it, Stein is also supported by Galaburda and they – including Nicolson and Fawcett – consider the cerebellum to be a key explanatory factor. I will explain in greater detail how these ideas can be connected to my own ones about automaticity, awareness and alternation between whole and parts.

Not many reading and dyslexia researchers have made explicit references to the philosophy or theory of science. One who has – and who has been a great source of inspiration for me – is Usha Goswami, first in the book she wrote together with Peter Bryant: *Phonological Skills and Learning to Read*, and later in many empirical and experimental works, where I have found practical examples of ideas that I first read about, and was inspired by, in Karl Popper's *The Logic of Scientific Discovery*.

Even if I have been inspired by the above-mentioned researchers – and many others – I have not discussed the ideas in this book with any of them.

As a result of my own studies in logic and the philosophy of science, I take a special interest in the definition of 'dyslexia'. There are two main issues in this context. First, the definitions used are very unclear and highly variable. This makes it difficult to compare findings across studies. Second, I consider it to be a major problem that several definitions include causal explanations. To this should be added that, in my opinion, answering the question of what dyslexia is must be seen as one of the most important tasks of research. This means that the concept of dyslexia must be seen as, and treated as, a hypothesis. I have tried to elaborate on the ramifications of this in one of the chapters of this book. That chapter is based on an article that T.R. Miles encouraged me very strongly to publish in *Dyslexia*, hoping that it would stimulate the elaboration of fundamental definitions.

Most people agree that comprehension is the most important goal of reading. However, since most reading research has been carried out in English-speaking cultures, insufficient attention has been paid to hermeneutics, which has developed mainly in Germany and France. Hermeneutics is an interpretive method which is applicable to everything from sensory impressions to the experience of existence. It can be seen as a parallel to the hypothetico-deductive method: the whole is confronted with the parts in an analogous way to how hypotheses are confronted with empirical data. A further similarity is that someone using either of these methods can never be sure of having attained the truth. Since I believe that hermeneutics is a useful method for reading research, I consider it better to talk in terms of 'interpretation' rather than 'understanding' – which implies that the correct answer has been found. Reading, as I see it, is above all an interpretive skill.

I have called my book *Can We Read Letters?* Some readers are bound to think that this title is too clever by half or overly polemical. In my opinion, however, it not only emphasises the question of what reading is, but also highlights an unfortunate element in the research tradition: a tendency to take an atomistic approach to reading. To this should be added that the subtitle – Reflections on Fundamental Issues in Reading and Dyslexia Research – provides more down-to-earth information about the content of the book.

The various chapters of the book represent twenty-five years of work. Most of them are reworked versions of previously published articles or book chapters, but there is also some entirely new material, namely a historical overview (Chapter 1: 'Historical Introduction') and a retrospective glance (Chapter 8: 'Concluding Reflections'). Chapter 2: 'Challenges in Cognitive Psychology' is based on an article entitled 'Options and Limitations of the Cognitive Psychological Approach to the Treatment of Dyslexia' which was published in the *Journal of Learning Disabilities* (Sage Publications, 1999, Vol. 32(5)). Chapter 3: 'Defining Dyslexia' is based on an article entitled 'How Can We Best Define "Dyslexia"?' which was printed in *Dyslexia. An International Journal of Research and Practice* (Wiley, 1998, 3(2)). Chapter 4: 'Defining Skills' is a nearly unchanged version of the article 'What Are Skills? Some Fundamental Reflections', published in L1 – *Educational Studies in Language and Literature* (IAMTE, 2011, 11(01)). Chapter 5: 'Reading Skill', Chapter 6: 'Reading Fluency' and Chapter 7: 'Reading Instruction' are English versions of chapters from a Norwegian-language book entitled *Å lykkes med lesing* ('How to Succeed with Reading') (Gyldendal Akademisk, 2014). I would like to express my particular gratitude to all of the publishers mentioned above for generously permitting versions of the various articles and chapters to be printed in this book.

As most of the chapters are based on independent publications, there is some overlap between them. They can be read separately, but I have also tried to order the chapters so that they make up a whole.

Last but not least I would like to thank the Director of the National Centre for Reading Education and Research, Åse Kari Hansen Wagner, who started the process that has led to this book in the context of the preparations for the Centre's twenty-fifth anniversary. Further, I would like to thank Professor Per Henning Uppstad at the Centre, who edited the selection and was in charge of relations with the publishers. He used to be my student, and we have had many a talk about matters relating to the chapters of this book. He and I have written the three chapters entitled 'Reading Skill', Reading Fluency' and 'Reading Instruction' together.

Finn Egil Tønnessen
Professor
National Centre for Reading Education and Research
University of Stavanger
Norway

ACKNOWLEDGEMENTS

First of all I would like to thank Professor Emeritus Torleiv Høien, who invited me into the field of reading research. Twenty-five years ago, he and I were the only researchers at the newly established National Centre for Reading Education and Research in Stavanger. Today, the Centre has about fifty employees in the fields of research, education, popularisation and administration.

Ever since our Centre was established, we have enjoyed a large network of contacts and collaborators both locally, nationally and internationally. We have participated in major collaborative projects within both reading research and dyslexia research. In the preface, I have mentioned some of those who have provided inspiration for the articles included in this book. I would like to use this opportunity to extend my thanks to some of our Nordic collaborators as well.

The late Professor Ingvar Lundberg of Umeå University – and subsequently of the University of Gothenburg – was a visiting professor at our Centre for several years. He acquainted us early on with new trends and new works in international research, and his broad knowledge, his great enthusiasm and his large network of contacts were of crucial importance to our research operations.

Professor Kenneth Hugdahl of the University of Bergen carried out studies of 'dichotic listening' among dyslexics in the early 1990s. His findings seemed solid enough, but their interpretation has been controversial. Those studies were an early source for my ideas about the importance to good readers of automatisation, attention and attention shifts. I am grateful for the inspiring way in which Professor Hugdahl acquainted me with research in that field.

Later on in the 1990s, Professor Heikki Lyytinen of the University of Jyväskylä became an important collaborator and inspirer. He showed that a large number of factors may influence reading skill and that early assessment and stimulation are crucial to reading development.

Professor Pekka Niemi of the University of Turku was affiliated with our Centre as a visiting professor. Whenever there was a conflict between fashionable schools of thought, he managed to be both open-minded and level-headed.

Professor Sven Strömqvist of Lund University also became a visiting professor and made a strong contribution to the linguistic competence and interests of the Centre.

A number of other people – both from Nordic countries and from further afield – have contributed inspiration, help and contacts in a range of fields.

Important assistance not only of a linguistic nature, but also to enhance the clarity of my works in the English language, has been provided in the form of translations by and critical comments from Johan Segerbäck.

I would like to thank all of those mentioned above – as well as all of those that there is not enough room for me to mention here. Even if these colleagues have meant a lot to me, they have no responsibility for the present product.

Financial support for the publication of the book has been generously provided by the Reading Centre and the Research Council of Norway.

HISTORICAL INTRODUCTION – BEGINNING AND CONTINUATION OF DYSLEXIA RESEARCH

INTRODUCTION

I here use the term 'history of *dyslexia* research', but as we will see there are various terms for, as well as various views of, the condition studied. While there is widespread agreement that dyslexia includes difficulties in both reading and writing, there is disagreement as regards how large those difficulties have to be, how prevalent they are and whether they change through development and/or pedagogical intervention.

Gough and Tunmer (1986) define 'the simple view of reading' as follows: Reading = Comprehension × Decoding. They assert that dyslectics are poor readers because of inadequate decoding, and this is a view that has become increasingly common. Someone with poor decoding skills will of course also have problems with comprehension. The term 'general reading difficulties' is often used about those whose problems are primarily with comprehension, as a result of factors such as low IQ, inadequate concentration ability or a limited vocabulary.

This brief overview is intended as an introduction to the subject for doctoral students in the field of special education. It is not possible to provide a complete or objective presentation of the history of dyslexia research. In this chapter, I have limited the selection of research contributions to those that I deem to have been particularly important. As a rule, many other researchers will have arrived at more or less the same findings or ideas, but if they were all to be mentioned the chapter would be reduced to a catalogue of names and studies. So would also be the case if I were to mention all those who have challenged the findings or ideas that I have chosen to include.

As regards the structure of the historical presentation, the choice is primarily between chronological and thematic organisation of the material. The most comprehensive and authoritative account published so far (*Dyslexia. A hundred years on* by Miles & Miles, 2001) chose the latter option, which gives a good overview but fails to show how ideas have developed and influenced each other over time. What is more, a given theme, theory or finding may mean different things in different historical contexts. In this chapter, my main organisational principle is chronological, but I will not emphasise the ways in which researchers have influenced each other even though I try to convey an impression of both change and continuity. I have not followed strict chronological order but gathered material thematically to some extent, above all in the section entitled 'Continuation'. I have divided the history of dyslexia research into two main periods – 'Beginning' and 'Continuation' (this division can and should be questioned, but not here) – with the transition in about 1960, when the volume of research increased markedly. There are a number of reasons for that increase: both schools, teachers and politicians became more willing to prioritise dyslexia research, and at the same time the 'Sputnik Shock' led to increased spending on schools, education and research in general. There was also an increased awareness of the importance of written-language skills for education, culture and participation in society. A further important development in this research field around 1960 was that the physicians lost their former dominant position to educationalists and psychologists, who progressively took on a more important role in dyslexia research and treatment.

The first part of the history, from about 1900 to about 1960, and the last one, after about 2000, are the least covered, for two reasons: During the first of those periods, there was relatively limited, but creative, activity. During the second, by contrast, activity has been more intense than ever before, but neither the creativity shown nor the changes occurring and the findings made have been proportionate to the efforts made. As the historian of science Thomas Kuhn has claimed (Kuhn, 1970), paradigms (or fundamental circumstances) of research change relatively rarely. Kuhn's term for research carried out within the framework of an established paradigm is 'normal science'. This involves researchers trying to falsify or verify each other's findings and making minor modifications. I would claim that dyslexia research has had a kind of established paradigm since the 1970s. First, this field has been dominated by cognitive psychology. Second, the main focus has been on phonological difficulties within dyslexia. These issues were clarified and subjected to more in-depth study over the two or three decades from 1970 onwards, and also supplemented with contributions from other fields, above all medicine, such as brain research as well as research into perception, motor skills and genetics. Then, for 10–20 years starting in the mid-1980s, there was a period characterised by creative and courageous hypotheses in these fields. In the past few years, however, normal science would seem to have been dominant. While the replication of other people's studies is obviously important and valuable, especially when the samples are larger and the studies are carried out with greater methodological rigour, it is not likely to yield many major advances that deserve mention in a brief historical overview.

In my presentation, I will focus specially on what dyslexia is and what the underlying causes are. By contrast, I will not devote much attention to the methods and tools used for purposes of evaluation, treatment and intervention.

In the present introduction, I will otherwise stress two main points. First, it is often difficult to compare research findings because the definitions used are unclear or different. Indeed, generally speaking, definitions represent a weakness present throughout the history of reading and dyslexia research. This aspect has been neglected or assigned insufficient priority. What is more, it is open to discussion whether the diagnostic methods and equipment used correspond to the definitions. On a related point of terminology, it is a controversial issue whether the word 'diagnosis' has too medical a ring to it – perhaps it would be better to talk about 'evaluation' and 'exploration', even if those words are not entirely suitable either.

The second point that I would like to stress is that, as regards explanations, it may be appropriate to make a distinction between causal mechanisms and aetiology. If, say, a person has difficulty linking language sounds to letters, this is a causal mechanism which explains certain symptoms in reading behaviour. Then it is obviously interesting to know why those abnormal causal mechanisms affect some people but not others. This may be due to a specific brain abnormity or injury, and it may also be due to genetic factors. Such neurological and genetic factors, then, are the aetiology underlying the causal mechanisms. In the literature, it is often difficult to determine whether researchers claim to have identified causal mechanisms or aetiological explanations.

Finally, I would like to say a few words about why researchers should take an interest in the history of their discipline. Knowledge for its own sake is one reason, which requires no further elaboration. Some may stress the aspect of usefulness: learning to avoid repeating the mistakes of others or to avoid re-inventing the wheel. Inspiration may be an even more important aspect: seeing how one's predecessors have had their victories and their defeats can be helpful in maintaining one's courage in the search for solutions and answers. Personally, what I find even more useful is the 'mental gymnastics' that an encounter with history forces one to engage in: when one makes one's mind follow a variety of lines of reasoning it has not before been exposed to, one is inspired to find and follow other new routes. Unlike Columbus, we may be rather well aware of where we have come, and we also know a little about where the roads lead from here.

BEGINNING

The ophthalmologist James Hinshelwood published an article in 1895 about a young boy who could not read despite having normal intelligence. According to Hinshelwood, this was due to an insufficient or inexistent ability to store visual impressions from print or writing. There were no shortcomings in the auditory field: 'the auditory memory being unimpaired and sometimes exceptionally good these children have no difficulty in rapidly learning to spell and will be able to spell words long before they have learned to recognise them by sight' (Hinshelwood, 1917, p. 106). It was controversial whether, and if so why, such a problem should apply mainly to printed or handwritten texts. Hinshelwood listed three types of reading difficulties: he used 'word blindness' about the greatest and most permanent problems; 'dyslexia' about minor and largely transient problems in beginning readers; and 'alexia' about those who had low intelligence – and the attendant problems with comprehension – in addition to difficulties remembering letters and written-word images. Based on the patients that he had recorded and examined, he asserted – as many have done after him – that the problem was the most prevalent in boys and men. Hinshelwood was of the opinion that the shortcomings of visual memory were innate, but even so he claimed that treatment could exert a positive impact, even though it could not entirely remove the problem (cf. the treatment scheme designed on this basis and published in several versions, such as Gillingham & Stillman, 1969).

Until about 1920 a series of British ophthalmologists took positions similar to the ones described above (e.g. Morgan). Then the centre of gravity of dyslexia research shifted to the United States. The US neurologist Samuel T. Orton influenced the direction of much of the research carried out in 1925–1950. While his predecessors had provided detailed descriptions of small numbers of cases, towards the end of his career Orton could refer to over 1,000 (there is even occasional mention of 3,000) children examined by himself. Like Hinshelwood, he considered that the causes of reading difficulties were largely to be found in the visual system, but he did not think the children lacked visual memory or were entirely 'blind' to letters and words. Rather, he was of the opinion that visual impressions were 'distorted' in the perceptual processing of letters and words, which is why he used the word 'strephosymbolia'. This applied in particular to the confusion of letters such as 'b' and 'd' (which he referred to as 'static reversals'), but also to changes in the order of letters, such as 'sun' being read and perceived as 'nus' ('kinetic reversals'). Like Hinshelwood, Orton considered that the problems were the most prevalent in boys and men. Further, Orton was of the opinion that the problems were hereditary.

Noticing that left-handers were over-represented among children with strephosymbolia, Orton assumed that the problems were primarily due to an abnormal 'division of labour' between the two hemispheres of the brain. As we will see later, this explanation for the causes of dyslexia was further developed in the 1980s (Geschwind, Behan, Galaburda). However, the symptoms that Orton emphasised strongly (the 'distortion' of letters and words) have had less importance assigned to them by later researchers, for two reasons: it has been claimed that these symptoms are not particularly prevalent, and also that they are in fact part of normal development in many children.

Even though Orton's diagnostic criteria and causal explanations have exerted only a limited influence, he has made a lasting impact both because of the attention he directed towards the problem and because of the large number of children he examined. What is more, such courageous and creative researchers and original thinkers as Orton are rarely seen. In the United States, the Orton Dyslexia Society was founded in his memory. It has subsequently had a large importance internationally and is now called the International Dyslexia Association. While the centre of gravity of dyslexia research remained in the United States, there were also a few important researchers in Europe, and particularly in Scandinavia, at this time. Both the Swedish physician Hallgren (1950) and the Danish researcher Hermann (1959) have had lasting importance for the study of the heritability of dyslexia.

CONTINUATION

Directions of research

From the early 1960s, dyslexia was no longer primarily a concern for the health-care services, but rather one for the schools. Educationalists and psychologists assumed a dominant position in dyslexia research. However, it is interesting to note that medicine was to make a forceful return in the 1980s.

In the 1960s, behaviourism lost its dominant position in psychology to cognitive psychology (or cognitivism) through what has been called the 'cognitive revolution' (cf., e.g., Baars, 1986). Cognitive psychology started making real inroads in dyslexia research in the 1970s. Behaviourism had placed its main focus on observable behaviour and disregarded the non-observable mental aspects. In addition, it emphasised sanction (negative emotions) and reward (positive emotions) in learning. Further important aspects were association and automatisation.

Cognitive psychologists, by contrast, were more interested in the mental, inner processes, considering that behaviourism over-emphasised 'blind', automatic learning. Instead they focused on conscious, controlled learning. 'Metacognition' became a key concept. Properly speaking, this means 'knowing about knowing' or 'awareness of awareness'; what it involves is being aware of and able to control one's learning processes.

Starting in the late 1980s, connectionism emerged as a new school of psychology. It is often presented as part of cognitivism, but it is probably closer to behaviourism or situated in between that and cognitivism. Unlike cognitivism, connectionism does not wish to use inner 'representations' or 'images'; and unlike behaviourism, it does not primarily concern itself with external, observable behaviour. Instead, it mainly wishes to observe the neurological phenomena or laws entailing that nerve cells can be more or less activated (rather than just either 'off' or 'on'). Connectionists claim that repetition increases the likelihood of activation (which is similar to behaviourism's theory of association). And, like cognitivists, they like to make charts of mental processes – but while the cognitivists' charts show a one-way flow from input to output, those of connectionists show traffic flowing to and fro among all elements. For example, there is not just a single route between the image of the written word and its meaning and pronunciation. It is often necessary to return to the context of a word. This shift between the whole and the parts has many similarities to the methods of hermeneutics (the study of approaches used to interpret and understand texts, situations or phenomena in general). To this should be added that connectionism has developed computer programs simulating or imitating how humans go about learning or performing specific tasks. One example is how children learn regular and irregular past-tense forms of English verbs – that is, how they learn to say 'went' (irregular) rather than 'goed' (regular). Many claim that connectionists' simulations of the reading process are closer to reality than cognitivists' representations using flow charts and dual-route models.

Definitions and subdivisions

There have been a great many debates about the definition of 'dyslexia'. The most commonly used definition was suggested by the World Federation of Neurology in 1968: 'A disorder manifested by a difficulty in learning to read despite conventional instruction, adequate intelligence and socio-cultural opportunity. It is dependent upon fundamental cognitive difficulties which are frequently of a constitutional character' (Matejcek, 1968, p. 22).

Taking that definition as a starting-point, the International Dyslexia Association (formerly the Orton Dyslexia Society) and others have taken the initiative in developing a new definition. Reid Lyon (1995) arrived at the following: '[Dyslexia] is a specific language-based disorder of constitutional origin characterized by difficulties in single word decoding, usually reflecting insufficient phonological processing. These difficulties in single word decoding are often unexpected in relation to age and other cognitive and academic abilities; they are not the result of generalized developmental disability or sensory impairment. Dyslexia is manifested by variable difficulty with different forms of language, often including, in addition to problems with reading, a conspicuous problem with acquiring proficiency in writing and spelling' (p. 7).

The British Dyslexia Association (1993) has proposed a broader definition which is more strongly influenced by practice: 'A specific difficulty in learning, in one or more of reading, spelling and written language which may be accompanied by difficulty in number work, short-term memory, sequencing, auditory and/or visual perception, and motor skills. It is particularly related to mastering and using written language – alphabetic, numeric and musical notation. In addition oral language is often affected to some degree'.

The main point of disagreement as regards how to define dyslexia has been the relevance of including intelligence. For example, Siegel (1989) asserts that there is no connection between IQ and phonological skills. According to Stanovich (1991), rather than demanding a discrepancy or difference between reading skill and intelligence, the definition should include a discrepancy between listening skill and reading skill: if a person understands much less by reading a text than by listening to it, this could be seen as a sign of dyslexia.

In the 1960s it became increasingly common to claim that what distinguishes dyslexics from other poor readers is a difference in degree rather than in kind. For example, some have preferred using the term 'delay' rather than 'deficit'. Those who think the difference is one in degree simply identify dyslexics as the bottom part of the normal-distribution curve; those who think there is a difference in kind claim that dyslexics instead make up a 'hump' towards the bottom end of that curve (which consequently loses its characteristic bell-shaped symmetry). Among those making the latter claim are Rutter et al. (1976), based on a large study carried out on the Isle of Wight. This distinction matters: if dyslexia is seen as reflecting a difference in degree, the interventions made tend to involve increasing the dose of regular initial instruction in reading and writing; by contrast, physicians seeing dyslexia as having physical and innate causes tend to consider pedagogical and psychological measures as less effective.

Critchley (1964) felt it was important to distinguish 'specific developmental dyslexia' from general reading difficulties. Later on he claimed that the best way to make that distinction was by using genetic analysis: 'We owe to genetics the most cogent single argument in support of the conception of a constitutional specific type of dyslexia among the miscellany of cases of poor readers' (Critchley, 1970, p. 89). The reason for general reading difficulties, according to Critchley, is weak intelligence – above all inadequate comprehension. However, the greatest and most permanent reading difficulties are those caused by phonological difficulties. Such difficulties, to the extent that they entail problems reading words, obviously lead to comprehension difficulties as well, but those are not primary in the way that they are for people with general reading difficulties.

The physicians dominating dyslexia research before the 1960s were mainly interested in finding causal explanations. The subsequent work of psychologists and educationalists helped bring about more detailed descriptions of dyslexics' reading behaviour. This, in turn, made it increasingly common to claim that there are several types of dyslexia. If this is the case, then an appropriate subdivision of dyslexics will obviously make it easier to adjust interventions to suit the needs of individuals. Based on the nature of the reading mistakes made, Vernon (1957) claims that there are three types of dyslexia: First, visual dyslexia, which corresponds to the problems that medical research had focused on. Second, auditory dyslexia, where the mistakes made suggest that the children lack correct connections between sounds (phonemes) and letters (graphemes). And third, inadequate capacity for abstract thinking, where the children affected are unable to analyse words of spoken language (the stream of speech) to identify individual sounds. Making a distinction between visual and auditory dyslexia became increasingly more common in the 1960s (cf., e.g., Myklebust & Johnson, 1962).

Boder (1973) took this tradition further but used the terms 'dyseidetic' and 'dysphonetic', where the main problem of those belonging to the former group is perceiving words as wholes while that of the members of the latter group is to associate phonemes with graphemes. Boder also had a third group: the 'alexic', who have problems in both areas. The Norwegian researcher Hans-Jørgen Gjessing asserts that he subdivided dyslexics in a corresponding way as early as in the 1950s (cf. Gjessing, 1977; Gjessing et al., 1988).

Mattis, French and Rapin (1975) identified a subgroup characterised by motor problems. A noteworthy point here is that the subgroups are described by reference not only to their reading or writing mistakes but also to symptoms in other fields. This may be relevant if such problems in other fields share their causes with the reading and writing difficulties – and it may make it possible to examine whether children are at risk of reading difficulties even before they first start school. For example, Nicolson and Fawcett (1990) have asserted that it is not enough to test for phonological difficulties, even though it is important to gain an overview over them. In their opinion, dyslexics also have problems with issues such as automatisation, motor control and conception of time.

Nicolson et al. (1997), using PET scans, found dyslexics to have lower activity than normal readers in the cerebellum, which plays a crucial role for tasks such as the regulation of movement. Denckla and Rudel (1976) claimed that the largest subgroup of dyslexics (more than 50%) have language problems that manifest themselves as difficulties with rapid automatised naming (RAN) as well as certain motor problems; another common reference for this position is Wolf (1979, 1984). Those who have both phonological difficulties and problems with RAN were seen as having a 'double deficit'. It was argued that having children undergo an RAN test before they learn to read could identify those at risk of reading and writing difficulties. Further, according to Tallal, dyslexics have particular problems with the rapid processing of information – and hence with the processing and perception of rapid and/or brief stimuli. Phonemes, especially consonants, require rapid processing. Tallal claimed that she was able to improve children's ability to perceive phonemes by first artificially increasing their duration and then progressively making them shorter (Tallal et al., 1997).

One interesting subdivision of dyslexics is that proposed by Bakker (1990): 'P-type' (perception) versus 'L-type' (linguistic). According to Bakker, the right hemisphere of the brain primarily perceives wholes. Dyslexics making use mainly of that hemisphere belong to the P-type. The left hemisphere primarily perceives details, and those dyslexics who rely mainly on that hemisphere belong to the L-type. Bakker asserts that good readers are able to alternate between the two hemispheres in an appropriate manner, such that they will sometimes focus on the whole and sometimes on the details.

Another common distinction is that between 'developmental dyslexia' and 'acquired dyslexia', the latter applying to people who have had normal reading ability but where this has been impaired as a result of brain damage, for example following a stroke (cf., e.g., Ellis, 1993; Coltheart et al, 1986, 1993). The symptoms exhibited by people with acquired dyslexia are much more heterogeneous, reflecting the complex nature of reading skill and the large number of things that may go wrong. Because of this diversity, there has been some opposition to categorising or subdividing acquired dyslexia, but even so three categories are often mentioned. First, 'phonological dyslexia', where one of the main symptoms is difficulty reading non-words. Second, 'deep dyslexia', which also involves semantic mistakes such as reading 'bus' for 'car'. Reading abstract words tends to be more difficult than reading concrete ones. And third, 'surface dyslexia', where the main problem is remembering and recognising whole words. Since each word is analysed and treated as a new word, the resulting reading pace is very low.

Frith (1986) claims that children go through three stages in their reading development. The first is the 'logographic' stage, where they see words as images or wholes without identifying the component letters. Examples include trademarks or logos such as 'Coca-Cola' that children recognise before learning the letters. The second is the 'alphabetic' stage, where children read each letter before arriving at the whole. The third is the 'orthographic' stage, where children know how to spell the words and have encountered them so often that they see both the whole and the letters.

Phonology – language

Alvin and Isabella Liberman, who worked at the Haskins Laboratories, were influential at an early stage in the school of research claiming that dyslexia is caused by phonological difficulties. Their colleague Donald Shankweiler has further developed their thinking. These researchers start not just from cognitive psychology but more specifically from cognitive psycholinguistics. In their opinion, dyslexia is primarily due to problems with spoken language – in particular, the ability to distinguish between and identify phonemes. As we have seen, earlier researchers were preoccupied with auditory difficulties that could, for instance, make it difficult to isolate and identify phonemes in the stream of speech. Placed in the context of cognitive psychology, such ideas gained new strength and influence.

Even though the Libermans and their colleagues claim that reading difficulties are due to problems with spoken language, they also assert that spoken language develops much more naturally than reading skill does, explaining why fewer people have problems with spoken language. They emphasise that reading is a late feature of our evolutionary history and that it is more artificial and more culture-specific. For example, children tend to perceive the word 'sun' as a whole which is primarily associated with a meaning. Many find it strange to break that whole up into the individual sounds /s/+/ʌ/+/n/.

Vellutino (1979) reviewed earlier reading and dyslexia research, concluding that the importance of visual factors had been both misunderstood and exaggerated. In his opinion, visual mixing-up of letters or words is rare. Moreover, where it does occur in beginning readers, those affected can be both normal readers and dyslexics. The reason for this is that the children's linguistic perception is still under development; if they mix up, say, 'd' and 'p', this is because the sounds are similar. According to Stirling and Miles (1988), unclear pronunciation is more frequent in dyslexics than in normal readers, which may be due to problems with auditory discrimination (cf., e.g., Brady et al., 1983). Snowling et al. (1986) added that this is also related to inadequate short-term memory.

Cognitive psychology introduced flow charts giving visual overviews of the elements and structure of cognitive processes. This tool was also used by cognitive reading research, where one model that has become particularly widespread is the 'dual-route model' (cf., e.g., Seymour, 1986). According to this model, there are two 'routes' from script to meaning and pronunciation. One of them leads directly from whole words to their meaning and pronunciation and is the one taken by good, fast readers. The other is 'indirect' in that it begins with a breakdown of the written image into individual graphemes. Then those graphemes are associated with phonemes, and finally those phonemes are brought together to form a whole. When that whole is associated with a word from spoken language, its meaning is perceived. At this stage, however, there may arise problems. If, say, the written word 'sun' is broken down into the phonemes /s/+/ʌ/+/n/, it is still not certain that this will be identified with the spoken word 'sun', for example if it is pronounced too slowly. It should be added that, even though this 'double route' was formalised and strongly emphasised by cognitive psychology, this idea can be found more or less implicitly throughout the history of reading and dyslexia research.

Morais et al. (1979) asserted that not only does phonemic awareness promote reading skill, but the activities of reading and writing also cause children to pay attention to the individual phonemes of their language. According to Goswami and Bryant (1990),

> it [i]s most unlikely that the progress that children make in reading is determined by their sensitivity to phonemes. On the contrary their progress in learning to read (or to read an alphabetic script at any rate) is probably the most important cause of awareness of phonemes. Children are not particularly sensitive to the existence of phonemes in words at the time when they begin to learn to read, and if they do not learn an alphabetic script they continue to be insensitive to these phonological units for some time. (p. 26)

Here it should be noted that there exist not only units that are larger than phonemes, such as syllables, but also ones that are smaller. For instance, a spectrogram will show that the sound representing the phoneme /a/ consists of several elements and that those elements manifest themselves in various ways in different linguistic contexts and in different people; relevant factors include age, sex, dialect and language. Further, at an intermediate level between phonemes and syllables are onset and rime. For example, the word 'strict' consist of one syllable, but that syllable can be divided into an onset: 'str' and a rime: 'ict'. Goswami and Bryant (1990) claim that these units are very important in children's acquisition of reading skill:

> The important phonological units for young children are onset and rime. The phonological skill that they bring to reading and writing is the ability to divide a word into its onset and its rime, and also to categorise words which have the same onset or the same rime [...] Our evidence suggests that right from the start, and perhaps with very little explicit instruction to do so, children learn to associate onsets and rimes with strings of letters. [...] One of the most interesting results of this early sensitivity to onsets and rimes is that children make inferences or analogies about new words on the basis of spelling patterns in words that they already know, and that they do this as soon as they begin to read. (p. 147)

The term 'phonological awareness' or 'phonemic awareness' is frequently used in dyslexia contexts, but what exactly does it mean? The definitions vary and are often unclear. The US National Reading Panel (2000) published a report called *Teaching Children to Read* based on a large selection of research projects and publications, which includes the following quotation on that subject:

Phonemic awareness (PA) refers to the ability to focus on and manipulate phonemes in spoken words. The following tasks are commonly used to assess children's PA or to improve their PA through instruction and practice:

1. Phoneme isolation, which requires recognizing individual sounds in words, for example, 'Tell me the first sound in paste'. (/p/)

2. Phoneme identity, which requires recognizing the common sound in different words. For example, 'Tell me the sound that is the same in bike, boy, and bell'. (/b/)

3. Phoneme categorization, which requires recognizing the word with the odd sound in a sequence of three or four words, for example, 'Which word does not belong? bus, bun, rug'. (rug)

4. Phoneme blending, which requires listening to a sequence of separately spoken sounds and combining them to form a recognizable word. For example, 'What word is /s/ /k/ /u/ /l/?' (school)

5. Phoneme segmentation, which requires breaking a word into its sounds by tapping out or counting the sounds or by pronouncing and positioning a marker for each sound. For example, 'How many phonemes are there in ship?' (three: /š/ /I/ /p/)

6. Phoneme deletion, which requires recognizing what word remains when a specified phoneme is removed. For example, 'What is smile without the /s/?' (mile) (p. 2.2)

In other words, 'phonemic awareness' is made into a very broad concept. The demands placed on the ability to concentrate and to think abstractly are great. Anyone who masters all of this is very likely to be good at decoding. But once the level of the various skills mentioned in points 1–6 above rises above a certain point, improvements in those skills will presumably no longer entail corresponding improvements in decoding skill as measured in reading pace and number of mistakes. To this should be added that there are very good readers who do not perform particularly well in those six areas. It can thus be questioned to what extent phonemic awareness is necessary for reading:

> [T]he utility of phonological abilities as predictors of reading development varies across different languages. For instance, while rhyming skill predicts learning to read in English (Bradley & Bryant, 1983), it is a poor predictor of subsequent reading achievement in German (Wimmer, Landerl, & Schneider, 1994) and Dutch (de Jong & van der Leij, 1999), where rapid naming ability accounts for larger proportions of unique variance in reading ability.

> Although there has been a burgeoning of research on dyslexia in different languages in recent years (Goulandris, 2003), cross-linguistic studies that directly compare dyslexia in English (about which we know a great deal) and dyslexia in a different language are still comparatively rare. Nonetheless, the

11

prevailing view is that the core phonological deficits of dyslexia are harder to detect in children who have learned to read in transparent orthographies such as German or Italian. (Vellutino et al., 2004, p. 17)

While many researchers claim that the existence of 'phonological' problems at the pre-school age is the best predictor of reading difficulties, Scarborough (1990) asserts that pre-school children who later turn out to be dyslexic have a normal vocabulary but use a restricted syntax. In other words, she considers that dyslexics show early signs of non-phonological problems.

Vellutino et al. (2004) recommend focusing on what works and what does not when it comes to teaching children with difficulties how to read, instead of trying to find out what their problems are – an approach whose net effect 'would be to shift to intervention as the primary means for defining the disorder' (p. 30).

Perception – motor skill – neurology – genetics

The early 1980s saw the start of work to further develop Orton's theories. Geschwind, Behan and Galaburda (1985) argued, like Orton had done, that the primary cause of dyslexia is an abnormal 'division of labour' between the two hemispheres of the brain. They also agreed with him that dyslexia is most prevalent in boys and men. However, they did not consider genetic causes to be primary. They focused mainly on the higher prevalence of left-handedness and immunological diseases in dyslexics than in the general population.

Since the specialisation of the brain hemispheres (which determines, among other things, hand preference) and the development of the immune system pass through critical stages at the same time in a foetus, these researchers assumed that abnormal physiological circumstances could be involved in both cases. In further work based on this hypothesis, special emphasis has been placed on the relative size of the planum temporale in the left and right hemisphere, respectively (the planum temporale is normally larger and more active in the left hemisphere; cf., e.g, Tønnessen, 1997b). New technology has also made it possible to study the activity (blood flow) of the planum temporale on either side of the brain (cf., e.g., Duane & Gray, 1991; Filipek, 1999; Pennington et al., 1999).

Simos et al. (2002b) examined the brain activity of eight dyslexics aged between seven and seventeen, finding that their patterns of activity during reading differed from those of normal readers. However, after 80 hours of training their activity was more normal. No certain conclusions can be drawn from this finding, but it could indicate that pedagogical approaches can affect the way in which the brain operates. By analogy, it could then be assumed that the absence of stimulation or the wrong type of stimulation could give rise to problems; it is likely that young people are the most susceptible to influence in this respect. And yet there are also many indications that dyslexics will have to wrestle with their problems throughout their lives (Vellutino et al., 1996, 2000). Many training or treatment approaches do seem able to help, but do they primarily alleviate symptoms or do they permanently affect the causes of the problems?

Stein and Fowler (1985) made two interesting claims: that co-ordination at motor level of the two eyes is a problem among dyslexics; and that dyslexics' eyes are not entirely stable during fixations. Subsequently, Stein and Walsh (1997) asserted that dyslexics also have problems with the magnocellular system, one of two main systems involved in vision (the other is the parvocellular one, centred on the pupil and the fovea, which is used during fixations to study details). The magnocellular system records wholes and movement. It determines, among other things, how the eyes should move about in a written text. It has since been claimed that there is a corresponding system in the auditory field. This means that it is possible to assert that the underlying causes of dyslexia are neurological in nature.

The difference between auditory and phonological difficulties is related to the fact that hearing is a general sense while phonology concerns the ability to distinguish and categorise language sounds. According to Eden and Zeffiro (1998), 'these perceptual and cognitive abnormalities arise from dysfunction of a neural system common to both'. Galaburda and Livingstone (1993) also support the idea that dyslexics' magnocellular system operates abnormally in both the visual and auditory fields. In the latter field, this entails problems processing and perceiving high-speed information (something that several others have also asserted, but using other causal explanations; cf., e.g., Tallal). Stein and Walsh (1997) claim that both the visual, the auditory and the motor systems are affected: 'the evidence is consistent with an increasingly sophisticated account of dyslexia that does not single out either phonological or visual or motor deficits. Rather, temporal processing in all three systems seems to be impaired. Dyslexics may be unable to process fast incoming sensory information adequately in any domain' (p. 147).

Since the 1980s, a steadily increasing number of sophisticated genetic studies of dyslexia have been carried out. One of the largest and best known was performed in Colorado, examining and comparing several thousand pairs of twins with and without reading difficulties (cf., e.g., DeFries et al., 1997). The study findings vary somewhat as regards the degree of heritability, but basically it has been concluded that genes and the environment are about equally important. Attempts have also been made to identify the key chromosomes, with above all numbers 1, 2, 3, 6 and 15 being mentioned. These findings, however, are based on probability estimates with considerable margins of error. Given the complexity of reading skill, and hence of reading difficulties, it is a reasonable assumption that additional genes and chromosomes play a part. For reviews, see Grigorenko (2001) and Fisher and DeFries (2002).

As mentioned, the first dyslexia researchers assumed that reading difficulties were hereditary. The rapid and extensive developments seen in medical genetics over the past 20–30 years give reason for hope that the key to early diagnosis will be found in that field. This could make early prevention and tailor-made interventions possible – but perhaps optimism has been excessive, for several reasons. First, there is a mismatch between imprecise definitions of dyslexia (see above) and the much more sophisticated and accurate methods and instruments used in genetics. This makes any results uncertain and subject to a variety of interpretations. Second, since reading is a complex skill, it is likely that several genes and chromosomes are involved to the extent that dyslexia is a hereditary condition. And third, the effects of genes and the environment in this specific case are uncertain. Certain characteristics, such as blood type, are hereditarily determined for life, but many others are determined by an interplay between the genes and the environment. And the recent branch of science called epigenetics suggests that the environment is in fact able to modify genes and their functions in the body.

It could be that other paths can take us further in terms of prediction, prevention and early, customised intervention. Heikki Lyytinen and his colleagues in 1993 began a large project based on the heritability of dyslexia. A large group of pregnant women were asked whether they or the fathers of their children had (or had had) reading difficulties. If one or both parents did, their children qualified for the study group. If neither parent had ever had any reading difficulties, their children instead qualified for the control group. Obviously, the definitions of reading difficulties underlying the assessment of whether the parents had had such difficulties represent a point of unclarity and uncertainty in this project, but the study design is still promising. Starting when the children were six months old, a series of tests were carried out. These were followed up frequently using age-appropriate tests until the children were of school age. Both in terms of the number of participants, the number of tests and the duration of the study, this is one of the largest projects carried out in dyslexia research. It is also one of the projects that have yielded the largest number of publications, and it has produced a number of findings increasing the predictability and preventability of reading and writing difficulties (cf., e.g., Lyytinen, 1995, 2002; Lyytinen et al., 2007).

Evaluation – intervention

I have chosen to use the words 'evaluation' and 'intervention'. Others prefer terms such as 'diagnosis' and 'treatment', but they may evoke medical precision and effectiveness. The definition of dyslexia is relatively imprecise, which makes it harder to operationalise the conditions that must be met, and also to find effective interventions. Still, it is remarkable how much the various methods used have in common, even though the causal explanations underlying them are different.

The past 30–40 years have seen the development of a series of new approaches to evaluating dyslexia. One of the best-known is the Bangor Dyslexia Test (Miles, 1997), which – besides traditional reading tests – includes questions as to whether the person is left- or right-handed and whether any member of the person's family has reading or writing difficulties. It is also tested whether the person has difficulty reciting the multiplication tables at a reasonable pace, whether the person has problems with tongue-twisters such as 'spectroscopy' and whether there are cases of letters being mixed up with each other.

In the Phonological Assessment Battery (Frederickson et al., 1997), the reading of non-words is the most important component. One sub-test involves children being given three words (such as 'sun', 'moon' and 'stone') and asked to identify those that begin with the same sound. It is also tested how quickly the children can name things and read numbers. In another sub-test, the children are to produce 'spoonerisms': if told 'Hong Kong', they should respond with 'Kong Hong'. The children's ability to find rhyming words is tested for example by having them decide which words among those presented – say, 'bone', 'book' and 'stone' – rhyme with each other.

The tests available have progressively become quite numerous. Another that particularly deserves mention is the Dyslexia Early Screening Test (Nicolson & Fawcett, 1995), which tests a range of motor skills – especially automatisation and co-ordination – claimed to be associated with later reading skill, on the assumption that the risk of reading difficulties can be determined to some extent at an early pre-school age.

When it comes to interventions, Hinshelwood (1917) made the following claim: 'My long experience of congenital word-blindness has enabled me to give with confidence a much more hopeful prognosis […] viz. that in nearly all cases […] the children so affected with proper treatment and great perseverance can be taught to read' (p. 90 f.). Hinshelwood used a 'multisensory' method, according to which the children should both see, hear and write the letters and words. Repetition and high-volume training are also important in this context. His method was called Simultaneous Oral Spelling (SOS); it has quite a bit in common with the 'look and say' method of the Whole Language school of reading instruction.

Orton (1937) claimed that 'the best approach and the one which yields the best return for teaching efforts is to find the smallest possible unit which the child can handle and begin a gradual reconstruction of the sequences or series of the smallest units'. (p. 218). In essence, this is the same as proponents of the Phonics school of reading instruction claim to this day. Orton's assistant Anna Gillingham further developed the treatment approach: 'The technique in this book is based upon the constant use of association of all the following – how a letter or word looks, how it sounds and how the speech organs or the hand in writing feels when producing it' (Gillingham & Stillman, 1969, p. 17). This is clearly rather consistent with Hinshelwood's methods, and later studies have indeed shown that these methods are highly effective (Bryant & Bradley, 1985, p. 130 ff.). As regards the choice of words, emphasis is placed on finding a progression where the most frequent and simplest words are used initially, and where rarer and more complex words are introduced by stages. A further development of this method can be found in Miles (1998), *The Bangor Dyslexia Teaching System.*

There has been much discussion about how and when the concept of phonemes should be presented in reading instruction. Many children find it hard to distinguish and identify phonemes in the stream of speech. Liberman (1973) studied 40 first-year students (aged 6–7) and found that 50% of them could find the boundaries between syllables (e.g., 'stu-dent') but only 17% could identify the three phonemes of a simple word such as 'sun'. According to Studdert-Kennedy (1991), '[i]t is a general rule of both phylogeny and ontogeny that complex structures evolve by differentiation of smaller structures from larger. Accordingly, we should not expect children to build words from phonemes as adults do: rather we should expect phonemes to emerge from words' (p. 16). In other words, it is easier to begin with wholes and split them up than to begin with the smallest elements and build larger wholes. The Whole Language school of reading instruction represents an extreme version of this position; there is some variation within this school, but many of its proponents put off teaching children to identify and recognise phonemes for a very long time (cf., e.g., Goodman, 1996). When it comes to the question of what 'language units' are the most 'natural', it should also be noted, as mentioned above, that Goswami and Bryant (1990) focus on the intermediate level between syllables and sounds, namely on onsets and rimes.

As regards interventions to prevent and remedy dyslexia, there are probably grounds for drawing a general conclusion to the effect that various versions of phonological training, repetition/'overlearning' and multisensory stimulation have been the most broadly used. However, there is some variation among the phonological approaches used. Adams (1990) notes the following about reading instruction in general:

> What if we restrict attention to the programs that are centered on phonics? Can we extract an operational definition of the endeavor from them? The answer is no or, at least, not easily. The problem is that there exist many, many such programs – each of Robert Aukerman's books cite over 100. To be sure, a central tenet of each of these programs is that working knowledge of the letter-to-sound correspondences underlying our system of writing is key to proficient reading. Beyond that, however, they differ greatly. (p. 51 f.)

Finally, when it comes to more untraditional and controversial methods, the Doman–Delacato method can be mentioned as an example. It was developed on the basis of neurological studies and theories. While it became very controversial in the context of dyslexia treatment, it remains in use to some extent in the treatment of certain other learning difficulties and neurological conditions. The idea was that dyslexia is due to abnormal development in parts of the brain, particularly the cerebellum (which Nicolson and Fawcett would later also associate with dyslexia). According to Doman and Delacato, those abnormal circumstances had arisen because the children had not gone through all stages of physical development in the right way. To attain 'full neurological organization', daily exercises including crawling, balancing, rhythmic movements, etc., were carried out for about a year (cf. Doman et al., 1960).

A FINAL NOTE ON THE HISTORY OF DYSLEXIA

In this chapter I have used a somewhat coarse division into 'beginning' and 'continuation', mainly to pinpoint the origins – or beginnings – of dyslexia research and to emphasise the characteristics of this research during the development of a paradigm in the 1960s and 1970s – the continuation. However, this division also reflects a claim on my part that knowledge about the beginning is important not only to understand the continuation but also to discuss and challenge the existing paradigm. The steady increase in activity within dyslexia research has made it even more important to ask questions about where we should go from here and what opportunities for new thinking and improvement are available to us. This requires us to ask a few fundamental questions and to examine and discuss alternatives – and that is precisely what I will try to do in this book.

CHALLENGES IN COGNITIVE PSYCHOLOGY

INTRODUCTION

From the turn of the century until the 1950s, it was commonly understood that dyslexia was a biologically determined condition. Perceptional and neurological anomalies were centrally featured in theories on the disorder. In the 1950s and 1960s it became increasingly common to attribute reading and writing difficulties to inadequate or incomplete education. Beginning in the 1970s, many began to ascribe the cause of dyslexia to a 'language disorder' – and especially to a deficient phonological awareness (cf. Vellutino, 1979). As described in the first chapter, most theorists in this tradition have taken a cognitive approach to language. As in other areas of cognitive psychology, flow charts, cognitive models and related ideas have played a central role in the study of dyslexia. The 'dual-route model' is a typical example (cf. Coltheart, 1978; Coltheart, Curtis, Atkins, & Haller, 1993; Ellis, 1993; Marshall & Newcombe, 1973; Morton, 1979; Seymour & Porpodas, 1980). These kinds of models have given us detailed information about the various sub-skills that constitute reading ability and, accordingly, about which sub-skills can create obstacles for individuals with dyslexia. However, when we try to use a cognitive approach to understanding why these individuals cannot accomplish all or some of the pertinent tasks, we see the limitations of this approach. Often, we seek explanations beyond it, looking, ultimately, for a biological explanation (e.g., Frith, 1997). If the field of cognitive psychology is to avoid the use of introspective methods, it must focus on the objective norms or rules for correct performance of cognitive tasks and not on subjective processes. In this manner, the cognitive approach will be more analytical, theoretical and logical than empirical. Cognitive psychology alone is not able to answer the question, 'Why is it that some people have difficulty following some of the cognitive norms or rules?'

In this chapter we analyse how cognitive psychology defines and treats dyslexia. We will also show how behaviourism and connectionism can function as supplements in areas in which cognitive psychology has displayed weaknesses and limitations.

SOME CHARACTERISTICS OF COGNITIVE PSYCHOLOGY

Cognitive psychology is to a large extent a reaction to behaviouristic 'black-box psychology'. For example, Morton and Frith (1994) proposed that we cannot understand autism without accepting a cognitive level between the biological and behavioural levels. Even though many cognitive psychologists would agree with this, the word 'cognitive' has taken on a wider definition than that which was originally intended within cognitive psychology. Morton and Frith apparently used the term to encompass most psychological or mental phenomena – including emotions, experiences and fantasies – whereas cognitive psychologists have traditionally used the term exclusively for intellectual and rational activities. We will see later how it is problematic to use the term as broadly as Morton and Frith did.

Traditionally, cognitive psychology has received important input from the fields of artificial intelligence and cognitive simulation. Two of the major players in these fields made this claim: 'There is a growing body of evidence that the elementary information processes used by the human brain in thinking are highly similar to a subset of the elementary information processes that are incorporated in the instruction codes of [...] computers' (Simon & Newell, 1964, p. 282).

It is important to recognise that there have been, and still are, differing opinions as to what cognitive psychology entails. For example, Battig (1975) made the following firm statement:

> What makes the current high popularity of cognition especially astounding is that even its most dedicated advocates seem unable to provide us with a clear or consistent definition of exactly what is meant by or encompassed under the cognitive label, or how it is to be distinguished from the allegedly non-cognitive character of whatever is (or was) not described as cognitive psychology. (p. 195)

H. Kreitler and S. Kreitler (1976) remarked that 'the term "cognitive" has been used so widely that one might wonder whether there is anything in psychology that is not cognitive' (p. 4). Despite conflicting opinions, a definite characteristic of cognition presents itself. Bechtel (1988) maintained that 'as the cognitive paradigm developed, the idea that cognition involved the manipulation of symbols became increasingly central [...] [The symbols] were enduring entities which could be stored in and retrieved from memory and transformed according to rules' (p. 1). Mental representations and rules are highlighted as characteristic features in historical presentations of cognitive psychology (cf. Flanagan, 1991; Gardner, 1985). 'Computability' is also a word that is often used; Von Eckardt (1993) referred to it in the following manner: 'The starting point of computability is the idea of an effective procedure – a set of rules which tell us from moment to moment, precisely how to behave' (p. 107). Further, it is worth mentioning the connection with computer science, on which Neisser (1976) elaborated:

> It was because the activities of the computer itself seemed in some ways akin to cognitive processes. Computers accept information, manipulate symbols, store items in 'memory' and retrieve them again, classify inputs, recognize patterns and so on [...]. Indeed the assumptions that underlie most contemporary work on information processing are surprisingly like those of nineteenth century introspective psychology, though without introspection itself. (pp. 5 and 7)

This last remark is important in light of the fact that there is some disagreement among cognitive psychologists concerning avoidance of the subjectivism in introspective psychology. As Cohen (1977) put it, 'We had a language to talk about what happened inside a man which was not a mentalistic introspective language, which was not hypothetical neurophysiology and which wasn't simply a description of the visible behavior' (p. 63). However, we can hardly avoid the introspective method if we expand the cognitive to include emotions and experiences as, for example, Morton and Frith (1994) have done.

Cognitive psychologists have tried to highlight the objectivity in their research by comparing cognitive processes to a computer program. Furthermore, the relationship between a computer program and computer hardware has been used to illustrate the relationship between the mind and the body. Knapp (1986) put forth that

it was possible to speak of a hardware and a software level, a very appealing metaphor for many psychologists long perplexed by brain-behavior relationships. Ever since, the prevailing notion has been that the computer, for the first time, gave psychology the concepts needed in order to develop a science of cognition, one that could stand independently from the science of physiology. (p. 14).

We will not take up the complicated mind–body problem here, but both research and everyday experience attest that this comparison fails on important points. In the case of humans, it is a fact that an organic injury to the brain can alter intellectual ability. It has also been shown that psychological problems can lead to permanent somatic damages. Yet, when we look at computers, a defect in computer hardware will rarely result in a defect to the software, even though damaged hardware will make it impossible to use the undamaged software. Along the same lines, damaged software will not normally cause permanent damage to the hardware. However, damaged software will make it impossible to use the undamaged hardware properly. This indicates that we must often define and solve problems related to learning and to other cognitive processes in a manner different from the way in which we define and solve problems that arise in computer hardware or software.

In delimiting the cognitive realm it is useful to borrow some concepts and distinctions from Popper (1977). He identified three worlds: World 1, World 2 and World 3. World 1 is the physical reality, which we can verify or falsify with the help of our senses. World 2 is the inner, personal reality of emotions, fantasies, experiences and thought. It is this reality that introspective psychologists investigate. If the definition of the term 'cognitive' is expanded as Morton and Frith (1994) would have it, we would to a large extent be using introspective methods. World 3 can be examined with more objective methods; this reality is available for thought but not for the senses. Here we find, among other things, mathematics and truths of logic. The rules for grammar in languages are also found here. For example, the linguistics of Chomsky (1966) can basically be placed within this reality, which is very reminiscent of the Platonic realm of ideas. It is clear that Schnaitter (1986) placed cognitive psychology within the realm of World 3 when he remarked that 'the information-processing mechanisms proposed in contemporary cognitive psychology are neither part of consciousness nor accessible to introspective scrutiny' (p. 295). Von Eckardt (1995) believed that cognitive psychology attempts to find the answer to the question, 'How does a normal, typical adult typically exercise his or her capacity [...]?' (p. 308). This can give the impression that cognitive psychology makes generalisations based on observations from World 2. What we understand to be correct and important in von Eckardt's statement is that cognitive psychology has a normative character in the sense that it describes the normal, or correct, way to deal with a cognitive task (e.g., reading).

The 'dual-route' model for reading (cf. Coltheart, 1978; Coltheart et al., 1993; Ellis, 1993; Marshall & Newcombe, 1973; Morton, 1979; Seymour & Porpodas, 1980) must be placed primarily within World 3. The central feature of the model is its definition of what reading is – or should be. It points to two main ways of reading, each of which is made up of several sub-skills. It does not deal with causal analysis; that is, it does not imply that some skills are the cause of other skills. It is primarily a logical analysis that attempts to (a) determine which sub-skills constitute higher-order skills and (b) logically order these sub-skills. For example, grapheme–phoneme associations cannot be made if we have not first identified the grapheme and the phoneme. Grapheme identification and phoneme identification are, in other words, a logical necessity for grapheme–phoneme associations. Because the alphabet is man-made, we must explicitly learn the grapheme–phoneme relationships. For example, when Liberman (1997) stated that it is not as natural to learn the written language as it is to learn the spoken language, this is a truism that follows from the definition of the alphabetic principle.

In World 3, we find a logical decomposition of the skills that take place in World 1 or World 2. Bechtel (1988) explained that this is an important difference between cognitive psychology and connectionism (PDP):

> This decompositional strategy lies behind traditional cognitive models, which quite naturally (given the decompositional approach) construe information processing as a matter of manipulating symbols according to rules. [...] But PDP models move radically away from this approach. Rather, the performance of the cognitive tasks is viewed as an 'emergent' product of quite different sorts of activity at the lower level. Components within the network send activating or deactivating signals to other components until the whole system settles into a stable state. It is the stable pattern of activation in the whole network that is then treated from a higher level as having a particular cognitive interpretation. (p. 146)

Insofar as cognitive psychologists involve themselves in the logical decomposition in World 3, it is necessary for them to maintain a sequential and linear model. Connectionism, on the other hand, describes mental activity in World 2. Contrary to World 3, World 2 is located within time and space and, therefore, has room for parallel (or simultaneous) processing. In World 2, it is possible for connectionism to speak of emergent properties in a manner that is reminiscent of Gestalt psychology. The debate between cognitive psychology and connectionism in the dual-route model (e.g. Coltheart et al., 1993; Seidenberg & McClelland, 1989) would have been far more informative if the distinctions between World 2 and World 3 had been taken into account. In this way, it would have been possible to differentiate between what was empirical and what was logical in their models.

COGNITIVE EXPLANATIONS?

It is misleading to speak of 'mental structure' or 'mental models' as long as mental phenomena are assigned to World 2. Structures and models belong to World 3. Important questions in World 2 are, How do we follow the norms that are found in World 3? and Why do some people have difficulty following these norms?

'Flow charts', 'cognitive maps' and similar ideas are important to cognitive psychology. However, these do not refer to causal relations. They do not say anything about which powers are pulling or pushing us from the start to the end of a process, or between 'input' and 'output'. If we are driving to a destination, having a map does not by itself get us to our goal. Some do not reach the destination because they have misunderstood what the goal is; others believe that the goal is not attractive enough to warrant the journey. Still others may have problems following the map because they do not comprehend the principles on which the map is based. Some have engine problems; others drive off into a ditch before they reach the goal. If we are going to help those who do not reach the goal, it is necessary, but not sufficient, to know at which point they are having difficulty. We also have to know *why* they are having difficulty.

A dual-route model with flow charts is useful because it can tell us which sub-skills we achieve and which we do not. To help someone who has a reading difficulty, it is, obviously, important to know if the problem is one of identifying phonemes, one of connecting phonemes and graphemes, one of tying phonemes together, or something else. With the help of a detailed flow chart, one can pinpoint exactly which skills are being performed correctly or incorrectly. It is important to note that while doing this, we do not localise elements or describe structures that exist on the inner plane (World 2). We are only able to determine which skills are not being achieved according to the norm (World 3).

A difficulty can be detected only in the realm of behaviour (World I) – first and foremost by recording the amount of time required and the number of mistakes made. If we begin to take into account mental factors (World 2), we risk attempting to explain something that is complicated (behaviour) with the help of something that is even more complicated (mental activity). It would seem that Bolles (1983) was correct when he said, 'Much of modern cognitive psychology seems to have much less interest in behavior as such and in the explanation of behavior than it has in the understanding of internal processes for their own sake' (p. 35).

SOME CHARACTERISTICS OF COGNITIVE TREATMENT

Skinner (1986) made this assertion:

> The appeal to cognitive states and processes is a version, which could well be responsible for much of our failure to solve problems. We need to change our behavior and we can do so only by changing our physical and social environments. We chose the wrong path at the very start when we suppose that our goal is to change the 'minds and hearts of men and women' rather than the world in which they live. (p. 89f.)

What characterises a cognitive treatment? Cognitive psychologists often use terms that belong to World 2, such as 'awareness' and 'metacognition'. They imply that we can monitor and control our internal processes according to the norms and rules of World 3. If the treatment of dyslexia is based on this approach, we come upon a problem that Skinner (1986) referred to: how can we alter the inner realm of another person? Individual differences and lack of opportunity for observation make this task problematic. Skinner did not say that the task was impossible, but he believed that time and energy are more efficiently used by concentrating on changes in behaviour (Skinner, 1984). Is not change in behaviour also the ultimate goal of cognitive psychology? Why does a deficit of some sort occur in, for example, phonological awareness? Is it an ability that is lacking, one that must be built from the bottom up? Or are the abilities there, but requiring knowledge of how they are put to use? Metacognition involves the idea of rising to a level above the cognitive processes in order to view and control them from the outside. If it is true that the cognitive processes occur in modules, as Fodor (1983) claimed, this kind of superior consciousness and control would be problematic. Is there a module which monitors, unites and co-ordinates all the other modules? In any case, this kind of approach places great demands on abstraction and concentration abilities. If a person has difficulty with cognitive tasks in one area (e.g., phonological tasks), it would be reasonable to assume that he or she would have even greater difficulty with metacognitive tasks in the same area. If metacognitive knowledge of phonology were introduced before phonology proper, and the method succeeded, it could be an indication that the students did not really have the fundamental difficulties we thought. Perhaps the problem was that the students simply were not using the abilities they possessed. If these abilities do exist, then the teacher should function as a 'midwife', in the sense that he or she assists in the 'birth' of the abilities. But what is the teacher to do if the required abilities in a specific area do not exist? Schnaitter (1986) presented the problem thus: 'Suppose that Jones stammers whenever he has to report to his boss. But over the weekend he has read a book on the power of positive thinking and enters Monday's meeting having resolutely made up his mind not to stammer. Yet he stammers anyway' (p. 312).

Premature metacognition is not the only thing that can create difficulties for the weakest students. Von Eckardt (1993) stated, 'The human cognitive capacities are sufficiently autonomous from other aspects of mind (such as affect and personality) that, to a large extent, they can be successfully studied in isolation' (p. 312). This kind of modular thinking (cf. Fodor, 1983) makes it difficult to find a connection between learning on the one hand and motivation, stimulation and reward on the other.

Both research and practical teaching experience indicate that teaching programmes with a cognitive element can be very effective for individuals with dyslexia (cf. Hatcher, Hulme, & Ellis, 1994; Lundberg, Frost & Petersen, 1988). However, we also find elements of other theories of learning in these teaching programmes. This makes it difficult to determine which effects are due to cognitive elements. In his presentation and analysis of teaching programmes for students with dyslexia, Thomson (1990) wrote that, among other things,

> a further agreed component of teaching a dyslexic is the idea of over-learning and over-teaching. Due to attentional, memorial and other difficulties, the dyslexic will need the same material presented over and over again using different modalities and tasks. He will not deduce or 'catch' the rules unless they are continually reinforced. (p. 208)

Here we encounter the behaviouristic terms 'over-learning' and 'reinforce'. They are difficult to explain on a cognitive basis. It would seem that these methods are used for more cognitive effects (e.g., 'catching the rules'). When cognitive psychologists use computer-assisted learning programmes, there seem to be comparable effects. Great amounts of training not only lead to automaticity but may also lead to understanding (cf. Wise, Olson, & Ring, 1997).

Thomson (1990) continued by adding that 'although authors differ slightly in their emphasis, most agree that some form of multi-sensory learning is required. Multi-sensory learning involves the integration of visual, auditory, tactile or kinesthetic modes, as in associating letters with sounds in writing' (p. 208). When this kind of element is woven into a cognitive training programme, it becomes increasingly difficult to determine which effects can be attributed to its cognitive elements.

Researchers working within the cognitive tradition have recently found reason to question cognitive treatment procedures and effects (cf. Blachman, 1997; Olson, Wise, Johnson, & Ring, 1997; Torgesen, Wagner & Rashotte, 1997). Aaron and Joshi (1992) put forth that 'modern research has cast much doubt upon the usefulness of learning rules for reading and spelling' (p. 131).

BEHAVIOURISTIC AND CONNECTIONISTIC TREATMENT

On the question of the purportedly rule-based nature of language, Skinner (1986) reminded us that

> until the time of the Greeks, no one seems to have known that there were rules of grammar, although people spoke grammatically [...]. But cognitive psychologists insist that speakers and listeners must discover rules for themselves. One authority, indeed, has defined speaking as 'engaging in a rule-governed form of intentional behavior'. [...] But there is no evidence that rules play any part in the behavior of the ordinary speaker. (p. 88)

Here Chomsky (1966) would protest, together with the majority of cognitive psychologists. They are correct in maintaining that we need rules, but only as norms within World 3. We need these primarily after we have taken action – in order to see if we have made an error. There can also arise instances of doubt that make us consult the rules before we have completed a plan. Connectionists have developed computer programs showing that it is both possible and natural to execute learning as well as performance without the use of rules. Both word recognition and past-tense acquisition can, for example, be explained without recourse to rules (McClelland & Rumelhart, 1981; Rumelhart & McClelland, 1982, 1986).

In its view of rules as opposed to laws, connectionism has more in common with behaviourism than with cognitivism. Rumelhart (1984) noted,

> It has seemed to me for some years now that the 'explicit rule' account of language and thought was wrong. It has seemed that there must be a unified account in which so-called rule-governed and exceptional cases were dealt with by a unified underlying process – a process which produces rule-like and rule exception behavior through the application of a single process. […] Both the rule-like and the non-rule like behavior is a product of the interaction of a very large number of 'sub-symbolic' processes. (p. 60)

Connectionism is often classified as a form of cognitive psychology (cf. Flanagan, 1991; Gardner, 1985). However, if we look upon mental representations and rules as central characteristics of cognitive psychology (e.g., Bechtel, 1988; Flanagan 1991; Gardner, 1985), it is more natural to treat connectionism in conjunction with behaviourism. Both behaviourism and connectionism are most concerned with World 1. Both emphasise that learning occurs primarily through changes to the nervous system. Neither behaviourism nor connectionism takes into account the difficult questions concerning the causal connections among the behavioural, cognitive and biological realms that lie in Morton and Frith's (1994) model. Because behaviourism and connectionism do not distinguish sharply between the cognitive and the biological, it is easier for them to explain how we learn 'through the body' and through practice. For example, when we learn to swim or ride a bicycle, we learn skills that are absorbed into the body. If instruction were to begin with a theoretical introduction to the body's buoyancy in water and gravity's effects upon the cyclist, we could not ensure success in the execution of these tasks. If the intellect is engaged first and remains dominant, it is probable that learning will be inhibited and that performance will be both rigid and uncertain.

Both behaviourism (especially Skinner's version) and connectionism are well suited to explaining the gradual improvement that occurs through repetition and training – especially through trial, error and gradual adjustment. It is also an advantage that these schools can explain the connection between learning on the one hand and motivation, stimulation and reward on the other. Behaviourism and connectionism can lead to teaching programmes that are less intellectualistic than those in cognitive psychology. As a conceptual framework, the latter seems more able to explain the flexibility, the subtlety and the ability to learn from experience, as well as the resilience to damage, that we see in real-life readers (cf. Rumelhart, Smolensky, McClelland, & Hinton, 1986). Cognitivism operates with a near-absolute binary division between right and wrong, normal and abnormal, on and off, 1 and 0, whereas behaviourism and connectionism can better account for the gradual shading of one condition into another.

Abilities, competence and skills, as defined here, are to a great extent based on what Reber (1993) called implicit learning and tacit knowledge. It is learning that takes place, and knowledge that exists, largely independently of awareness of both the process of acquisition and the content of the knowledge so acquired. Classic examples of this are the acquisition of language and the process of socialisation whereby individuals come to speak their mother tongue and become inculcated with their society's norms, respectively, without conscious knowledge of the underlying principles that guide their behaviour.

A COMBINATION OF TRADITIONS

Aaron and Joshi (1992) wrote, 'Regardless of the method and setting chosen, it should be remembered that reading is a skill and, like any other skill, improves only with practice. In other words, to become a skilled reader, children have to read and read' (p. 122).

We believe that the term 'skill' requires a more closely defined and central place when it comes to discussion of learning and performance in reading. Learning to read involves something beyond learning to break the alphabetic code and to make correct grapheme–phoneme associations. What do we mean when we say that we can read? It does not mean that we can read all words with equal ease and certainty. We will always be able to read familiar words more quickly and with more certainty and fewer errors than we read unfamiliar words. One defining feature of skilled reading is being able to tackle both familiar and unfamiliar words.

Every skill presupposes an ability to switch between awareness and automaticity. The skill of walking is, to a large extent, characterised by automaticity when we move in one direction over an even surface, without turns or traffic factors. If we begin to *think about* walking, it is most likely that our movements become slower and more unsure. If the path is uneven, winding and traffic-laden, we must use more awareness to avoid a misstep or an accident. This example shows that three types of problems can arise: (a) insufficient automaticity, (b) insufficient awareness, and (c) insufficient ability to switch between the two in a flexible and expedient manner (cf. Tønnessen, 1997).

Automaticity is an important term within both behaviourism and connectionism. With regard to reading, it is the principal component of efficient decoding. For achieving maximum speed, minimal mistakes, maximum confidence and minimal effort in the decoding process, automaticity is a necessity. This liberates the greatest amount of effort, which can then be used in understanding the text.

We have seen that *awareness* is a central term within cognitive psychology. However, it has been used in a rather imprecise way. Reber (1995), in fact, pointed out that it has a wide range of meanings: 'The term has a long history which has found it being used to refer to a wide range of subjective phenomena from simple, primitive detection of very weak stimuli to deep understanding of complex cognitive and affective events' (p. 79).

Because it refers to subjective phenomena, awareness belongs to the realm of World 2. As mentioned, it is difficult to see how we can describe and explore this world in an objective way. It is also difficult to see how we can draw a boundary between World 1 and World 2 without hampering the 'communication' between them. In this respect, connectionism would seem to offer a more realistic and fruitful solution than cognitive psychology, as the former does not draw any clear-cut line of demarcation between the mental and the biological. One unanswered question, however, is whether connectionists make room for consciousness and awareness in a traditional sense.

One series of studies has indicated that awareness is necessary for decoding (cf. Adams, 1990; Liberman & Shankweiler, 1979; Lundberg. Olofsson & Wall, 1980; Olson, Forsberg, Wise, & Rack, 1994; Share & Stanovich, 1995). Automaticity is also necessary for reading (cf. Fawcett & Nicolson, 1994; Nicolson & Fawcett, 1990; Yap & van der Leij, 1993a, 1993b, 1994). However, neither of these is sufficient.

An important characteristic of good reading skills is the flexible shift between automaticity and awareness. During text reading, this corresponds to the alternation between familiar and unfamiliar words. Referring to computers that are able to 'read' with the help of scanners and synthetic speech, some may put forth the idea that we do not need awareness. Perhaps, in the future, cybernetic programs will make these reading machines just as self-governed and self-directed as humans. But we cannot put these programs into a human! Why should we try, when we can complete the task so well with the help of awareness?

OPTIONS AND LIMITATIONS

If cognitive psychology is to avoid the introspective method, it must concentrate on standards for correct performance of the cognitive tasks. This primarily involves a logical analysis of the tasks. If we search in the mental realm for an explanation as to why individuals fail to meet those standards, we cannot avoid the introspective method. If we are going to explain varying abilities in learning and performing, behaviourism and connectionism are better platforms.

In a treatment context, cognitive methods risk placing too great a burden on students' intellectual skills. The sharp division between cognitive skills and activities on the one hand and emotions, drives and needs on the other makes it difficult to integrate motivation in the learning process. In this case, behaviourism and connectionism have clear advantages, in that they do not perceive a sharp division between the cognitive and the biological. Furthermore, it is fortunate that they place so much emphasis on the behavioural level, as it is reading behaviour that all are engaged in improving!

Reading is a skill that requires a flexible and functional combination of automaticity and awareness. Behaviourism and connectionism seem to provide the most adequate explanation of automatisation. Cognitive psychology has provided important information on which sub-skills are needed for reading. However, many questions remain when it comes to awareness and metacognition, which ensure that the processes occur in accordance with the norms for correct performance. Can cognitive psychology describe and explore these mental processes without recourse to introspective methods?

DEFINING 'DYSLEXIA'

INTRODUCTION

Back in 1995 I took it as an encouraging sign that the very first issue of *Dyslexia – an International Journal for Research and Practice* included an article by Elaine Miles that asks the question, 'Can there be a single definition of dyslexia?' (Miles, 1995). The history of science includes many instances in which the formulation of daring or fundamental questions opens up new lines of development. The probability of this happening as a result of Miles's article is only increased by the fact that the author balances her criticisms with a good measure of constructive thinking, and that she invites further discussion instead of precluding it: 'The description given in this case would obviously be more tentative as its purpose would be to start a discussion'.

Miles's article may perhaps best be understood as one of several recent attempts at questioning the paradigm that reading research has been operating within. The extensive debate that the Orton Dyslexia Society has had concerning the question of definition would be another example. When such an influential organisation poses so many fundamental questions, then the chances are high that we will see some effect in our research and practice (cf. Lyon, 1995). This chapter aims to suggest guidelines and criteria for how we should formulate and evaluate definitions of 'dyslexia', and carries the conclusion that proposed definitions should be formulated and treated as hypotheses.

DIVERSE NEEDS AND PURPOSES

Miles (1995) refers among others to Elliott (1990), who notes: 'What is needed in Britain is an agreed definition of specific learning difficulties which carries some legal force'. If we are to achieve the ideal of equality under the law, we need some permanence, we need to make sure that the laws are clear, and that there is a consensus as to which children are to be labelled 'dyslexic'. Moreover, teachers will need to be given definitions of reading disorders that tell them specifically what they should be looking for in a child's reading pattern. Definitions that depend on complicated tests and procedures are of little use to teachers.

In addition we may mention that there is an ongoing power struggle, or at least a set of conflicting interests, transcending the needs of the various professional groups. Stanovich (1992) notes:

> Some definitions serve scientific purposes and can be judged by research criteria. But definitions of learning disabilities serve other purposes as well. They have been used by school personnel as a mechanism to leverage school

services for low achieving students. Additionally, definitions have been used by parents' groups as advocacy tools to force legislative recognition and to direct attention and resources to certain groups of children. [...] The highly restrictive definitions of the research community are resisted by school personnel, who often want the broadest definition possible in order to allow themselves discretion in providing services for children with generic school learning problems. (p. 279)

Science must seek truth. But that does not mean that it should remove itself completely from practical concerns. Yet in the long run, truth is both practical and useful. Research must not merely buy into the definition that is most current, for there is never any guarantee that the majority is right. Research needs to show creativity and critical good sense. Many people would concur with Fletcher et al. (1989) when they claim that

Careful analyses of the criteria used to define and select children with reading disabilities are urgently needed. There is a persistent tendency on the part of researchers and professionals working with this population to accept traditional definitions of reading disability based on consensus or professional opinion without examination of the assumptions or empirical characteristics of various definitions. (p. 334)

The terminology used in reading research has been both unclear and inconsistent (see for example Kavale and Forness, 1992; Lyon, 1995; Stanovich, 1994). Stanovich (1994) seems to feel a frustration at the lack of clarity in the use of the term 'dyslexia' when he notes: '[...] "dyslexia" carries with it so many empirically unverified connotations and assumptions that many researchers and practitioners prefer to avoid the term [...] (p. 579). He goes on to ask a question:

Thus the research literature provides no support for the notion that we need a scientific concept of dyslexia separate from other, more neutral, theoretical terms such as reading disabled, poor reader, less-skilled, etc. Yes, there is such a thing as dyslexia if by dyslexia we mean poor reading. But if this is what we mean, it appears that the term dyslexia no longer does the conceptual work that we thought it did. (p. 588)

Lyon (1995) claims: 'Despite the significant role that a definition should play in the scientific and clinical understanding of dyslexia, the field has constructed numerous vague, ambiguous, and non-validated descriptions of the disorder' (p. 4). Here we find a major cause of the disparate findings concerning the extent and cause of dyslexia. The bewildering varieties of terminology make it difficult to compare the results one researcher arrives at with the results another researcher has obtained. And fuzzy definitions also create problems in diagnostic practice. Establishing a clear and consistent terminology is one of the most practical and useful tasks a science can perform.

TRADITIONAL DEFINITIONS

There are a great many definitions of 'dyslexia'. The differences among them are not merely verbal; on the contrary, they also exhibit a great variety of ways of constructing definitions and of purposes for doing so. In an earlier article (Tønnessen, 1995), I tried to show that the definitions of 'dyslexia' may be grouped according to three principles on which they are constructed: (1) the symptom principle, (2) the causality principle, and (3) the prognosis principle. Most of the definitions that have been offered are a combination of (1) and (2). When it is claimed, for example, that one of the most important characteristics of dyslexia is persistence of dyslexic problems despite pedagogical assistance (e.g. Frith, 1981; Berninger and Abbott, 1994), then this would be a definition based on the third principle, the prognosis of the disorder. This principle could also be termed the 'effect principle', because it defines the disorder on the basis of the effect of the treatment. These effects may be seen at either the level of symptoms or the level of causes, but definitions based on prognosis are still not merely combinations of definitions based on the principles in (1) and (2). Because most of the proffered definitions have been based mainly on symptoms and causes of the disorder, I will briefly present and discuss the most well-known definitions based on principles (1) and (2).

The symptom principle

I use the term 'symptom' here in its broadest sense, referring to observable and/or measurable signs of underlying conditions and processes. When we describe reading behaviour or reading achievement without reference to their underlying causes, then we are at the symptom level. The most important symptom-based definitions are the 'discrepancy definitions'.

Most definitions of 'dyslexia' refer to a discrepancy between observed and expected achievement (see for example Shaywitz, Fletcher, & Shaywitz, 1995). The expected achievement is usually based on the pupil's IQ. Stanovich (1994) writes that

> The critical assumption that was reified in these definitions – in almost total absence of empirical evidence – was that degree of discrepancy from IQ was meaningful: that the reading difficulties of the reading-disabled child with reading-IQ discrepancy (termed specific reading retardation in the classical investigation of Rutter and Yule, 1975) were etiologically and neurologically distinct from those characterizing the reading-disabled child without IQ discrepancy (termed general reading backwardness in the Rutter and Yule, 1975 study). (p. 581)

After examining a series of studies, Stanovich concludes: 'There is no indication that the nature of processing within the word recognition module differs at all for poor readers with and without IQ-discrepancy' (p. 587). Several recent studies have also come to similar conclusions (Fletcher, 1992; Fletcher et al., 1994; Olson et al., 1989; Siegel, 1989; Shaywitz et al., 1992).

Another type of symptom-based discrepancy definitions, which I find somewhat less problematical, are those that are based on a discrepancy between reading and listening comprehension (see for example Aaron, 1989). Yet even here I see some problems. First of all, this definition does not allow accurate and reliable measurements that make it possible to compare precisely these two modes of understanding texts. Secondly, the point of the definition would seem to be the assumption that the only difference between listening comprehension and reading comprehension lies in the word-identification process. A discrepancy between them should therefore be due to a deficient word-identification skill. This inference is problematical, however, since oral communication contains information that is not available in a text, such as intonation and prosody. A third problem with this definition is that some studies suggest that dyslexics do not solely have problems with written language, but with spoken language as well (see for example Johnson, 1994; Scarborough, 1990).

The discrepancy definition that would seem to be the least problematical is that based on the discrepancy between reading age (RA) and chronological age (CA). But the problem with this type of definition is that it does not define a closed group: the group can vary radically as to type of symptom and cause. How heterogeneous the group is depends on how broadly the reading tests that are used to define the RA are designed. The size of the group depends on how big a discrepancy between RA and CA one chooses as the cut-off point.

Lyon (1995) claims that 'These difficulties in single word decoding are often unexpected in relation to age and other cognitive abilities' (p. 15). Statements such as 'unexpected underachievement' and the like are often found in articles based on discrepancy definitions. I think these expressions are unfortunate, because it is often our lack of knowledge that makes the underachievement 'unexpected'. We may be lacking diagnostic information about the 'unexpectedly' poor reader, or perhaps our field has not gained enough insight into the causes of dyslexia.

The causality principle

The difference between a symptom and its cause is often arbitrary. Geschwind and Galaburda (1987) claim, for example, that an elevated level of testosterone during certain weeks of gestation can cause abnormal brain lateralisation, which in turn can cause learning difficulties and left-handedness. In this model, one could say that abnormal lateralisation is a symptom of too much testosterone during pregnancy. I think, however, that we should reserve the term 'symptom' for the final link in the causal chain – in this case, learning difficulty and left-handedness.

The most common definition based on the causality principle is the 'definition by exclusion'. The World Federation of Neurology, for example, defines 'dyslexia' as 'a disorder manifested by difficulty in learning to read despite conventional instruction, adequate intelligence, and sociocultural opportunity. It is dependent upon fundamental cognitive disabilities which are frequently of constitutional origin' (cf. Critchley and Critchley, 1978). A great many studies of dyslexia have done their sampling by excluding pupils who did not meet these criteria. At root in this definition is an assumption that these factors are not the cause of dyslexia. There is a serious deficiency, however, in this line of reasoning. Even if we assume that dyslexia is of constitutional origin, this does not disallow the fact that there are some dyslexics who have grown up in a pedagogically or socially impoverished environment, or who have lower–than-normal intelligence. Originally, these groups were excluded on purely methodological grounds, in an attempt to make sure that the condition being studied was not caused by an impoverished environment or deficient intelligence. But by excluding these groups from the sample, we have given the sample a lamentable bias. Serious objections to exclusionary definitions have been raised, on both theoretical and empirical grounds (see for example Fletcher & Morris, 1986; Moats & Lyon, 1993; Stanovich, 1993).

There are many studies which indicate that dyslexia has a constitutional origin (e.g. Cardon et al., 1994; Galaburda, 1991; Hynd & Semrud-Clikeman, 1989; Wood et al., 1991). In my opinion, however, causal factors should not be included in the definition until such time as they have been precisely described and thoroughly verified. I do not think any of the causal explanations we have today meet this criterion. In order to avoid unnecessarily constricting the research into the aetiology of dyslexia, it is important that our definitions are based solely on symptoms.

A great many studies show an association between dyslexia and an impairment in phonological processing ability (see for example Adams, 1990; Brady & Shankweiler, 1991; Gough, Ehri, & Treiman, 1992; Liberman & Shankweiler, 1979; Liberman, Shankweiler, & Liberman, 1989; Lundberg, Olofsson, & Wall, 1980; Olson, Wise, & Rack, 1994; Share and Stanovich, 1995; Stanovich, 1993; Vellutino, Scanlon, & Tanzman, 1994; Wagner & Torgesen, 1987). It is often unclear whether the phonological anomalies are considered as being symptoms or causes. Lyon (1995), for example, claims that reading difficulties are 'usually reflecting insufficient phonological processing' (p. 9). Here it seems to me that he is claiming that the phonological deficit is the cause of the reading problems. Despite the wealth of data indicating an association, I still feel that this association should be treated as a hypothesis that should be made more precise and formally verified before it is brought into a definition of 'dyslexia'.

CAN WE DEFINE 'DYSLEXIA'?

Miles (1995) asks the question, 'Can there be a single definition of dyslexia?' This question needs to be treated both theoretically and empirically. For example, there are studies indicating that the symptoms can vary from person to person, and also from situation to situation for the same person (see for example Moats, 1994). Moreover, if one feels that dyslexia is a syndrome consisting of a series of more or less vague symptoms, then it will be very difficult to arrive at a precise definition of the disorder. This will also be the case if it is true, as claimed by Ellis (1993) and others, that 'reading backwardness seems to be a graded thing more like obesity than measles. We cannot in any simple way divide the population into those who are dyslexics and those who are not, so it would seem unlikely that there will exist any symptom or sign which will qualitatively distinguish dyslexics from non dyslexics' (p. 111). (See for example Shaywitz & Shaywitz, 1994; Stanovich & Siegel, 1994.)

Why do some researchers feel that dyslexics and normal readers differ only in the degree of ability, while other researchers feel that there is an essential difference between these readers? Why do some claim that dyslexics can be delimited as a group, with a clear set of characteristics, while others claim that this is impossible? The reason for the disagreement is in part empirical: they have discovered different patterns in their findings. But why have they found different patterns? One reason is that they have been focusing on different things. Another reason is that they employ different assessment procedures and instruments, and that they sample in different ways. All of these differences can in part be traced back to the variety of definitions of 'dyslexia' that the researchers have been using. Empirical facts and theories, in my opinion, are so intimately woven together that we can never decide which theory is right solely on the basis of one of them. In this article I hope to make the case that theories and empirical findings ought to be bound together by treating any definition of 'dyslexia' as a *hypothesis*.

WHAT TYPES OF DEFINITIONS?

Any attempt at defining something raises many theoretical and in particular logical issues. We are able to examine only a few of the more fundamental of these. In the classical tradition from Plato and Aristotle to the early Wittgenstein (Tractatus Logico-Philosophicus), any term can be defined by a finite list of criterial features, so that any member of the class displays these features and non-members do not. The later Wittgenstein (Philosophische Untersuchungen), and a series of subsequent philosophers, logicians, linguists and psychologists have distanced themselves from the classic view of definitions. Instead, they have emphasised the fact that categories in the real world tend to have fuzzy boundaries and blend into one another. Wittgenstein claimed that objects which share the same name (normally) exhibit a 'family resemblance'; that is, they do not share one or more definitive characteristics, but rather a network of resemblances, like persons whose faces share features characteristic of a family. In logic, this view has been deepened and systematised in the field of 'fuzzy set logic', which deals with degrees of membership in a class (see for example Zadeh, 1975). In psychology, we find something similar in Rosch and Lloyd (1978), who claim that words and concepts are best defined and learned through the use of examples ('stereotypes' and 'prototypes'). From an anthropological point of view (e.g. Geertz, 1983) we find the notion that the possibility remains that the most crucial questions about categorisation may continue to elude cognitive–scientific methods.

Of course it is difficult to know to what degree these questions can be answered theoretically or empirically. It seems, however, that the classical thinking about definitions works best with natural phenomena. Anything properly termed 'gold', for example, has an atomic weight of 197 and a melting point of 1063°C. Terms used for man-made phenomena, for example 'democracy', are less amenable to classical definitions. Even though this difference between naturally occurring and man-made phenomena is useful, it does not solve all the problems. For example, it is debatable whether the way in which we divide the spectrum of visible light (red, blue, etc.) is natural or man-made (see for example Berlin & Kay, 1969; Heider, 1972; Sahlins, 1976). To what degree other psychological phenomena are natural or man-made is also a matter of dispute. Behaviourism, for example, has tried to find a maximum of natural phenomena in psychology. Because many of the classic versions of cognitive psychology have been based on the model of the computer, we find that many of the central terms used in this school are amenable to classical definition. Connectionism, however, has preferred a more 'fuzzy logic' type of definition based on stereotypes and prototypes (cf. Flanagan, 1991).

Miles (1995) claims that '[…] "description" may be a better term than "definition" […]' (p. 37). Well, that would depend on how we define 'definition'! It is common practice to speak of a term's meaning as one thing, and its reference as something separate (see for example Lyons, 1977). 'Meaning' is a linguistic phenomenon, 'reference' is not. If I am to provide the meaning of the word 'bachelor', I do so by saying that it is equivalent to the meaning of another linguistic expression, in this case, 'unmarried man'. This is called an 'intentional definition'. The word's reference, on the other hand, is the class of all unmarried men. An 'extentional definition' consists of a list of all the concrete examples that fit the category (see for example Salmon, 1973). Let us say that after performing an empirical examination I find out, just to continue with this example, that bachelors are self-centred, miserly, shy, introverted and suffer from overly strong attachment to their mothers. This would be a description of the reference of the word 'bachelor'. It would not be a description of the word 'bachelor'. What we need is a definition of the word and a description of the word's reference.

We also need to be clear about the difference between lexical and stipulative definitions. The former is used when there is wide agreement as to what a word means and how it is used. A 'triangle', for example, has the lexical definition: 'a closed plane figure bounded by three straight lines'. But a word like 'democracy' is not as amenable to lexical definition, because there is no widely accepted understanding of it. Therefore, when we want to use the word in a scholarly way, we need to make a stipulative definition of it. Here we can choose between the various existing definitions, or construct our own. In reading research we will have to deal with stipulative definitions; few, if any, of our thorny terms have good lexical definitions. By way of an answer to Miles's question, 'Can there be a single definition of dyslexia?', I would claim that there is no lexical definition of 'dyslexia'. In the following I will, however, suggest guidelines for stipulative definitions.

DEFINITIONS AS HYPOTHESES

The questions of how and if we can define 'dyslexia' must, in my opinion, be determined by both empirical findings and theoretical reasoning. In order to attend to both of these, we need to treat definitions as hypotheses.

Many researchers would gladly escape the burden of defining their key terms, not only because of the extra work that honing a precise definition entails, but also because they feel the need to keep the question open for as long as possible, so as not to restrict the research. Openness is of course a virtue in research. But some basic choices simply have to be made. Openness rather manifests itself in one's ability to change one's mind when the evidence indicates that one is wrong.

Any serious researcher needs to delimit and identify the phenomenon to be studied. If you want to select a sample of dyslexics, you need to know what identifying traits dyslexics share. What is the common denominator that permits us to group these people together under the label 'dyslexics'? What must they have in common, and which variables may vary from individual to individual? T.R. Miles (1994) speaks of 'lumpers' and 'splitters': '[…] lumpers being those who wish to group certain things together, and splitters those who wish to emphasize their separateness […]' (p. 195). In this context, he points out that '[s]ince boundaries often need to be changed as science advances there is no need to fan the flames of controversy by insisting that a particular boundary is the only correct one to draw' (p. 196). The answers you give to these questions will govern your choice of instruments and methods to be used in identifying potential dyslexics.

The temptation is to use a loose, fuzzy definition. This temptation should be avoided, however. In my reading of the history and philosophy of science, I think it nearly always proves to be the case that a maximum of clarity and precision in the definition of key terms is the best route in the long run. This means that the definition should be operational: 'The central idea of operationism is that the meaning of every scientific term must be specifiable by indicating a definite testing operation that provides a criterion for its application' (Hempel, 1966). An example: 'In order to ascertain whether the term "acid" applies to a given liquid – i.e., whether the liquid is an acid – insert a strip of blue litmus paper into it; the liquid is an acid if and only if the litmus paper turns red'. Even though many would object that operational definitions in psychology and education cannot be as precise and well-grounded as in this example, I would none the less claim that this should be our ideal, in the sense that it determines the direction of our work.

A good operational definition of 'dyslexia' will have to stick to symptoms. First of all because a definition has to have a high degree of intersubjective observability (i.e. we have to agree that these children present the symptoms, while the others do not). And second, because it is important that we do not define 'dyslexia' on the basis of notions as to its cause or causes. Definitions involving causal factors beg the research question by anticipating the results. Any research based on a definition of 'dyslexia' that outlines its causes will not really be empirical and a posteriori. For example, if you define 'dyslexia' as 'difficulties in reading non-words due to a deficit in the phonological processing', then you cannot really be studying the cause of the disorder, because you have already decided for yourself what it is. In fact, we find a distressingly similar phrasing in the new definition put forward by the *Orton Dyslexia Society*: '[...] difficulties in single word decoding, usually *reflecting* insufficient phonological processing' (Lyon, 1995, p. 9; my emphasis).

Looking back at the contributions made by many researchers in the history of our field, we often have to ask: which findings are merely true by definition and which are truly empirical findings? Assume, for a moment, that we define 'reading' as mainly decoding, and then define 'decoding' as phonological processing. Should we then be surprised when we find a high correlation between 'reading difficulties' and 'phonological difficulties'?

The American Psychiatric Association (1987) claims that it is both possible and desirable to delimit the symptoms before searching for the causes: 'The approach taken in DSM-III-R is atheoretical with regard to etiology or pathophysiologic process, except with regard to disorders for which this is well established and therefore included in the definition of the disorder' (p. xxiii). A similar stance towards delimiting and explaining disorders is fairly widespread in medical research. An example from medical history would be the delimiting of the concept of 'cancer' from purported causes of the disease (cf. Riese, 1953; von Engelhardt & Schipperges, 1980).

In order to allow a definition to guide and perhaps even inspire research, instead of circumscribing it too narrowly, we will have to treat the definition as a hypothesis. This is in accord with the notion of ontological relativity that is fairly widespread in the fields of logic and the philosophy of language (cf. Passmore, 1985; Quine, 1969). When we devise definitions in our field of research, we should not be too concerned about finding the one and only true definition. That may not even exist. We should instead be trying to devise the definition that best suits our purposes. That does exist. The only problem is, how do we know that we have found it? It is kind of like the top of the foggy mountain that surely is there, but which you cannot see. And even when you are there, you cannot be sure you are there.

Which symptoms should we start with? I think the answer is: only a very few, clearly delimited, and highly quantifiable ones. We need to find out whether or not these can be grouped together by studying whether or not they have a common cause or causes. The symptoms and causes selected must, in other words, reciprocally delimit each other. Or, to put it in the terms geneticists use, the genotype and the phenotype have to mutually define each other. When we have successfully delimited a cluster of symptoms that somehow 'belong' together, we follow the same route to find new clusters. Then we have to find out whether it would be advantageous to give each of the clusters of symptoms a unique name, and/or whether two or more clusters ought to be grouped together under the same name.

We need, in other words, to construct the concept of 'dyslexia' from the bottom up. First we need to find the individual building blocks, and then to find out what kind of edifice we can construct from them. This means that we have to first identify the various forms of reading difficulty and then ascertain whether their differences, similarities and associations indicate that they should be grouped together under the concept of 'dyslexia'. As I have claimed elsewhere, '[a]n inductive approach to subgrouping should be taken, and not the deductive approach that has been common in the literature. […] In this way the concept of dyslexia can be constructed from the ground up – if dyslexia exists' (Tønnessen, 1995, p. 153). We need, then, to start with the symptoms, and when we find the causes, then these may be drawn into the definition (cf. the above-mentioned DSM system).

I took it as a positive sign of the times that, for example, the Orton Dyslexia Society wanted a 'new, research-based definition'. But it is difficult to see how this can be reconciled with the same society's claim that 'the definition must be theory driven' (Lyon, 1995, p. 7). I am sceptical about this if by 'theory-driven' it is meant that the researcher is shackled by theories or paradigms. The scientist must remain free to choose new hypotheses. These are for the most part the products of creativity (see for example Popper, 1963), and creativity should be nurtured by both theory and empirical facts. The subsequent verification or falsification of the hypotheses ought to be based on observations that are as objective and as independent of theory as possible. I prefer an 'atheoretical approach' in this meaning of the word, such as DSM-III-R employs in its definitions of psychiatric disorders (American Psychiatric Association, 1987, p. xxiii). I propose that we need to work as empirically as possible by using the hypothetico-deductive method. Naturally, we have good reason to wonder if science ever can be wholly objective or 'neutral'. But dispassionate objectivity should be our goal, even if it is like the foggy mountain top we cannot see but know is there.

Moreover, traditional theories of reading have often had a normative aspect. They tend to postulate an ideal of effective reading. I think having a theory-driven definition will wind up defining 'dyslexia' as a deviation from this ideal way of reading. Instead of postulating some ideal way of reading, we ought to focus on normal reading. This should be done by a statistical registration of observable reading behaviour. Then we can profitably look for patterns of reading that deviate from this statistical norm. In this way we are assisted by our definition of 'normal reading' in identifying the clusters of symptoms I mentioned above in connection with definitions as hypotheses.

As mentioned, the definition should present the meaning of the word, e.g. 'bachelor = unmarried man'. Then empirical study can be carried out of individuals that fit the category, here 'unmarried men'. By means of such empirical study we may find that the subjects are, for example, self-centred, miserly, shy, introverted and suffering from overly strong attachment to their mothers. In chemistry we can say for example that everything to be included in the concept of 'gold' has to have a melting point of 1063°C. In psychology, however, we cannot demand that all of the characteristics should be identical in order for an instance to be included within the concept. But even though this is not possible, we should have it as the ideal towards which we strive. If there are meaningful differences in the characteristics, then we ought to see if we can delimit the group better, perhaps through subgrouping.

In the literature we find many symptoms which are more or less correlated with dyslexia (see for example Bannatyne, 1971; Miles, 1993; Wheeler & Watkins, 1979). This may indicate that it would be wise to delineate 'primary' and 'secondary' symptoms. 'Primary symptoms' would be core symptoms which are present in nearly 100% of the cases. 'Secondary symptoms' are not as frequent, but are still more prevalent in dyslexics than in normal readers. Through my own research into the associations between dyslexia, left-handedness and immune disorders (Tønnessen et al., 1993), I would for example consider left-handedness and immune disorders to be secondary symptoms of dyslexia. Further study may, however, prove these rather to be primary symptoms of a subgroup of dyslexics. Anyway, accompanying symptoms or conditions ought not to be included in a definition nor in the diagnosing of dyslexia, until such time as they have been proved to be a trait common to dyslexics or to members of subgroups of dyslexics.

Another interesting constellation is found in Fawcett and Nicolson (1994). In my interpretation of their material, I think it would here be correct to term the dyslexia itself as a symptom. This does not bar them from saying that dyslexia itself also has symptoms: 'The explanation is in fact markedly different from that put forward by phonological deficit theorists, especially with respect to specificity. Rather than accepting that the skill deficits are specific to reading-related skills, we propose on the contrary, that the reading related deficits are merely the tip of an iceberg, and that almost all primitive skills (such as speed of processing and motor skill) are likely to be impaired' (p. 184). If this is correct, then it is doubtful whether one ought to say that dyslexia is 'language-based'. Of course, dyslexia is also a language problem to the degree that reading difficulty is a problem with written language. But this is so obvious that I doubt that it needs to be accounted for in a definition.

DEFINITION AND SUBGROUPING

There is an extensive literature on the subgrouping of learning disorders (e.g. Miles, 1994; Feagans, Short, & Meltzer, 1991; Rourke, 1985). Looking at this literature, one has to wonder: have the researchers created an intractable problem for themselves? If we, like Plato, start out on the plane of pure ideas or notions, then we will have difficulty in finding our way back to earth. On the other hand, if we, like Aristotle, start out here on earth, then the experiences we have will show us how high up we can reach towards the pure ideas that Plato started out with. An example will illustrate what I mean. Let us say that we first observe a series of different animals. Then we try to group them in some way. We construct for example the concept of 'dog' by grouping Cocker Spaniels, Collies, Great Danes, etc., together. We do not proceed the other way round, by starting off with a vague and intuitive notion of 'dog' and then trying to find out how we can divide it into different subgroups. The whole question of the subgrouping of dyslexics has arisen because we have not been working empirically and inductively, but rather deductively and intuitively! An empirical theory of knowledge forces us to know the subgroups before we can know the group. When, for example, Boder (1973) delimits and identifies 'dysphonetic' and 'dyseidetic' dyslexia, we have to ask whether or not these subgroups have so much in common that they can profitably be grouped together under the name 'dyslexics'. What is their common denominator and what are the differences between the groups?

Miles (1994) claims that

> an attempt at an improved classification was made by Rutter and Yule (1975) when they drew a distinction between 'reading backwardness' and 'specific reading retardation'. Whether this classification has any long-term taxonomic power, however, may be doubted. […] It is arguable that they were thereby using only a weak taxonomy when a stronger one was in fact available. In scientific research caution is sometimes a virtue, but one may tentatively suggest that in this case it may have inhibited progress! (p. 207)

It is also my opinion that we ought to try to establish as small and clearly delimited groups as possible. We do not need to decide the issue of how or whether they are to be bound together. Others can do that, depending on their purposes and interests.

In my opinion, one cannot decide a priori which symptoms or which causes belong together. The symptoms need to be delimited by associated causes and the causes have to be delimited by their associated symptoms. We should start with the symptoms manifested by poor readers, say the 10% at the bottom of the ability scale, and then describe these individuals as objectively and clearly as possible. Stanovich (1994) claims that '[t]his problem is a recurring one in the field of developmental disabilities, and it arises because the field has repeatedly displayed a preference for terminology that connotes unverified theories about causation' (p. 579). Miles (1994) makes the further claim that 'disagreements over the concept of dyslexia are in effect disagreements over the issue of lumping and splitting' (p. 204). I concur. But these disagreements can also be traced back to what the purpose of the concept 'dyslexia' is. In part, this is a question of what the core of the concept should be. However, it is also a question of how precise a definition needs to be and how large a group it should encompass (e.g. the extension of the definition).

HOW CAN WE BEST DEFINE 'DYSLEXIA'?

Researchers have been working on dyslexia and reading problems for about a hundred years now, and we still have not reached a strong consensus on how to define 'dyslexia'. We need clear and useful definitions. We do not necessarily need only one definition to be used in all circumstances, just as we do not necessarily need only one hypothesis for everyone who wants to do serious research. What we need is a common goal and a set of common guidelines for how to define 'dyslexia'. We have reasonably clear criteria for evaluating research in general; what we need is a set of criteria against which we can evaluate proposed definitions. We need these criteria in order to be able to compare the various proposed definitions with an eye to sorting the wheat from the chaff. In fact, given today's circumstances, I am not even sure that the definitions we favour today are any better than the definitions formulated by our field's pioneers.

In summary I will propose the following guidelines: (1) We need to decide which goals and purposes are to be covered by the definition. We also need to decide whether we are to employ the term 'dyslexia'. (2) We have to try and find criteria by which we can ascertain whether one definition is better than another. Some guidelines are offered in the following. (3) We need to delimit the phenomena at the level of symptoms and not refer to causes until they are empirically verified. (4) In order to ascertain which of the symptoms are of most interest, we have to start with a description of the symptoms common to the poorest readers (perhaps the poorest 10%); this description should be as open, objective and clear as possible. (5) We hypothesise that a certain group of symptoms belongs together and verify this by ascertaining whether or not they share the same causes. We thereby obtain a set of symptoms that belong to a set of causes. This constitutes a subgroup. (6) We similarly define as many subgroups as it takes to cover all the symptoms which are typical among the poorest readers. (7) Two or more subgroups can be grouped together in a larger concept which we can then, for example, term 'dyslexia'. In this way we can construct the concepts from the bottom up. (9) One must always keep an open mind about new symptoms and causes, and about new ways of describing known symptoms and causes. (10) The concept of 'dyslexia' is given status as a hypothesis, which we should expect to be increasingly fine-tuned in accordance with ongoing empirical research. In order to verify, falsify and adjust the concept as expeditiously as possible it needs to be formulated precisely and operationally.

The guidelines I have proposed should not be considered final nor complete. Many will find them too strict or restrictive or too much like the hard sciences or medical science in particular. I agree with Miles (1995) when she claims that 'difficulty in formulating does not necessarily imply that one is talking nonsense' (p. 42). And, I would add: clarity is not enough! The difficulty in formulating is, however, one of the greatest challenges in our research. Many other fields have weathered similar definitory crises, and through persistent and systematic work they emerged stronger and wiser. I feel that all sciences, whether they study hard things, like chemicals and rocks, or soft things, like us, must strive for terminological precision, intersubjectivity, and well controlled, comparable and communicable results. These are the ideals that have pushed the envelope in field after field. No one can know beforehand to what degree we will be able to attain these ideals, but the history of science shows that aiming too high is better than aiming too low.

DEFINING 'SKILL'

INTRODUCTION

When the concept of 'skill' is used in reading and writing research or more generally in linguistic research, it is rarely made the subject of detailed and precise definitions or reflections. This chapter is a theoretical contribution that consists mainly in reflections on the type of phenomenon that 'skill' represents. Philosophically, the account is based above all on Aristotle's views, according to which 'skill' is characterised as a potentiality. Psychologically, this chapter expresses the opinion that the only way to describe, understand and explain 'skill' is by combining behaviourism and cognitivism.

CHALLENGES

Background and goals

Behaviourism and cognitive psychology have been two of the most influential schools in psychology in the past 40 or 50 years. In many ways they have been polar opposites and mutually exclusive. As an introduction I will examine the consequences of employing these disparate schools strictly and consistently. (In practice, researchers usually do not do this; most research being done mixes in some of the notions from the other camp. But this type of eclecticism is often more problematic than 'pure' models. Here I have chosen to use pure models primarily to make my line of argument easier to follow.) The reflections presented below have emerged from my work in reading research, but I would contend that they are also relevant to a number of other fields of research within psychology, education and linguistics. The aims of this chapter are (1) to focus on the fundamental problems of reading research; (2) to problematise the dominant position achieved by cognitive psychology in reading research; and (3) to call attention to the fact that the concept of 'skill' needs to be more closely defined and assigned a more prominent position in reading research. I will try to determine the philosophical status of 'skill' and try to define 'skill' by combining key concepts from both cognitive psychology and behaviourism.

PROBLEMS

Behaviourism ad absurdum

Behaviourism deals exclusively with observable behaviour (Watson, 1930). It is useful for describing associations between observed stimuli and observed responses in humans and in animals. It cannot, however, explain the messy deviations in our behaviour that are the result of our cognition or will. Moreover, this school of psychology cannot describe, much less explain, 'inner' phenomena such as doing sums in your head. If we exclusively base our science on observed behaviour, we will have to admit that there is quite a gap between the task someone is to perform and the solution he or she finds. For example: A voter in an election has to decide whether or not the promises the various candidates give during their campaigns are believable or not. Basing his or her vote on the candidates' observable behaviour alone would not be wise. A psychology that excludes non-observable entities such as thoughts and feelings will be a vastly limited science.

The principle of association between stimulus and response is fundamental to behaviourism's theory of learning. To create strong and lasting associations, repetition is necessary. The term 'overlearning' is used for when we continue with repetitions past the point when stable associations are established. Behaviouristic theories of learning do not traffic in notions such as 'understanding' (Leahey, 2001).

Heartbeats and breathing are for the most part automatised (that is, they take place without learning, but we can learn to regulate them somewhat). The term habit is used for actions we learn to perform. Habits are basic elements in behaviourism. But we should also note that habits can be affected consciously; we can change them by intellect and will. From this we may conclude that behaviourism alone is not sufficient for explaining all psychological phenomena.

Cognitivism ad absurdum

In cognitive psychology all attention is directed towards the 'inner' life (von Eckardt, 1993; Gardner, 1985). Traditionally this school focuses on 'thought' and 'awareness'. These terms, however, are unclear. Nor is it clear how thoughts, being very subjective things, can be studied. What are the 'causes' of our thoughts?

Behaviourism, as mentioned, uses overlearning in order to secure the best possible learning. For example, overlearning is a technique often used with dyslexics. Despite the fact that some cognitive psychologists and educators use this technique, it must be pointed out that this concept has no basis in their theory of learning; it belongs in the school of behaviourism. A pure cognitivist would have to employ cognitive techniques in working with dyslexics. The cognitive solution to dyslexia is cognition of cognition: metacognition (Gombert, 1992).

Metacognition makes great demands on intellectual ability and awareness – even for people without learning difficulties. An example: There is a widespread consensus that dyslexics have difficulties identifying and distinguishing phonemes. They thus also have difficulty forming correct associations between phonemes and graphemes. However, explaining this to dyslexics using metacognition is no easy task. In fact, it is somewhat akin to using intellectual reasoning to explain to a colour-blind person what colours are. Moreover, there is a question as to what is meant by this 'metacognition' (and by similar expressions such as 'awareness of awareness'). A subject cannot simultaneously be an object. An eye cannot see itself. Metacognition, as it is currently conceived, cannot be studied scientifically, nor can it be taught explicitly.

Assuring the quality of one's metacognition would require meta-metacognition. Assuring the quality of that would require meta-meta-metacognition – and so on, in an infinite sequence of ever more 'metas'.

In the real world there are no thoughts that are entirely unaffected by feelings, urges and sudden insights. This is an important reason for why a pure cognitivism is indefensible. Another problem with pure cognitivism is its inability to explain why we 'choose' one thought over another. The history of science shows that new ideas or discoveries often are arrived at by irrational routes (Kuhn, 1970). This can only be explained by granting some efficacy to feelings, urges and sudden insights. The same is true when we try to explain *mistakes* in reasoning and *learning difficulties*.

The problems involved with using the concept of metacognition to explain how the mind works do not collide with the obvious fact that we do monitor our own mental activities. Even if we cannot observe our mental activities while they are taking place, we can observe their *results*. Aquinas claims that 'the soul is known by its acts. For a man perceives that he has a soul and lives and exists by the fact that he perceives that he senses and understands and performs other vital operations of this kind [...] No one perceives that he understands except through the fact that he understands something, for to understand something is prior to understanding that one understands' (*De veritate*, 10, 8, Thomas Aquinas).

Cognitive psychology has often employed flow charts that illustrate the 'normal' paths followed in solving cognitive problems (Reber, 1993). The dual-route model of reading is an example (Coltheart, 2005). There has been disagreement about the usefulness of this model for describing, understanding and explaining 'normal' reading and reading difficulties; cf., e.g., Coltheart, 2006). Is this model best conceived of as a 'summary' of how people read? Is it a hypothesis about what happens at the neurological level or at the psychological level? Perhaps the most obvious way of understanding this model is to view it as a description of what is *meant* by 'reading'; that is, as a *definition* – more precisely, a *normative* definition that points out the necessary components of adequate reading. In such definitions there are more or less explicit conditions on what is 'normal' or effective reading. To the extent that these conditions are correct, 'flow charts' with their different 'boxes' may show us, for example, what 'subtasks' create problems for dyslexics. In this way they may contribute to a more precise description of dyslexia. Flow charts, however, do not give an overview of the *causes* behind the putative fact that reading takes place in a particular way. Nor do they give us any explanation as to how or why a particular instance of a person's reading is influenced by the situation or trial conditions. It should also be noted that flow charts do not give explanations as to how reading ability is developed. Therefore they do not tell us how to help poor readers. We have to know something about feelings, urges, habits, environmental factors and the like in order to understand how and why individual variations in reading ability (and in particular instances of reading) occur. Neurology, behaviourism and connectionism will provide more insight here than cognitive psychology.

SOLUTIONS

A realistic psychology

It must be concluded that pure behaviourism and pure cognitivism both lead to unreasonable consequences. An eclectic mix of the two is equally problematic. In the real world, body and mind make up a unified whole – but not a mixture. It is not so much the case that we *have* a body and a mind, but that we *are* both body and mind.

Models that simply assume an interaction between the biological/neurological substrate and cognition are riddled with the same problems that Descartes' *dualism* faced (cf., e.g., Frith & Blakemore, 2005).

The best hypotheses in this area are those developed by connectionism. Connectionism assumes as a starting point that there is no essential difference between the cognitive level and the neurological/biological level (Bechtel & Abrahamson, 1991).

One objection to connectionism, however, is that it ignores the differences between 'outer' and the 'inner' of mental acts. Ludwig Wittgenstein claimed that 'the human body is the best picture of the human soul [...]' (Wittgenstein, 1953, II, pp. iv, 178). He argued that (1) we have a consciousness that cannot be observed by others; and (2) mental activity cannot be taken as the *cause* of observable behaviour. He claimed, for example, that when you see someone 'break out in joy', their observable behaviour is a *criterion* or a hallmark of their inner joyful feeling. (Wittgenstein, 1953, §580). This is to say that both the mental and the physical aspects are part of the definition of 'joy'. A metaphor for this would be a mountain-top with two sides. Neither side can be said to *cause* the other. When we have seen both sides of the mountain, we can identify it more precisely and confidently than if we had only seen one side of it. Even if a mountain-top has several sides, we may use only one name for referring to the top. Similarly, the single term 'man' may refer to both an outer and an inner 'side'. Brain-imaging and other studies have given us much new knowledge about the brain, but the relationship between the mind and the brain as well as the definitions of, say, 'skills' or 'intelligence' are primarily philosophical problems and tasks that cannot be solved by means of brain imaging; cf., e.g., Brook and Mandik (2004).

Letting this notion of a mountain-top inform our thinking further, we can say that the relationship between the mental and the physical aspects of something, that is, between the 'inner' and 'outer' aspects of it, is like the relationship between a conceptual definition and an operational definition. The notion of 'intelligence', for example, can be operationalised by defining it as the score achieved on a certain test. Yet according to this way of thinking, we cannot say that the subject's intelligence *caused* him or her to achieve that score. It is often claimed that an operational definition is *logically deduced* from a conceptual definition. But it is not possible to deduce outer, physical manifestations from inner, mental activity. Rather, these phenomena are complementary; they shed light upon each other. In order to understand what is meant by, for example, 'reading', it is necessary to take into consideration both the outer, physical aspects and the inner, mental ones. Only when the phenomenon 'reading' is determined from both perspectives can we begin to look at causal relationships.

What are skills?

Just as a human being is a unique combination of mind and body, both of these aspects are reflected in the term 'skill'. In order to understand this term, we do well to look to Aristotle's philosophy. On the one hand, Aristotle disagreed with the materialists and the determinists, who claimed that all of our actions are the product of inherited factors and the pressures of the environment (nature *and* nurture). On the other hand, he rejected the claims of Socrates and Plato that as long as we *think* correctly, we will also *act* correctly. For them, a true philosopher is one who has clear and true thoughts; as such, he will also be a morally good person. Aristotle considered that Socrates and Plato put too much store in the power of thought in daily life. He held that intelligence and knowledge alone were not sufficient to lead a person to act in accordance with moral norms. In the real world, our actions are often some-what 'distorted' by feelings and bad influences. We need therefore to *practice* 'acting good' – but not as a 'mechanical' habit. On the contrary: we need to both follow general rules and at the same time take into consideration that which is unique in each situation. We acquire an *attitude or disposition* and thereby become virtuous (cf. Thomas Aquinas', 2006, distinctions between 'potentiae' and 'habitus' in *Summa Theologiae*, vol. 22, Ia2ae, pp. 49–54).

Regarding the acquisition of skills, Aristotle writes: 'of all the things that come to us by nature we first acquire the potentiality and later exhibit the activity (this is plain in the case of the senses; for it was not by often seeing or often hearing that we got the senses, but on the contrary, we had them before we used them, and did not come to have them by using them); but the virtues we get by first exercising them, as also happens in the case of the arts as well. For the things we have to learn before we can do them, we learn by doing them, e.g. men become builders by building and lyre players by playing the lyre; so too we become just by doing just acts, temperate by doing temperate acts, brave by doing brave acts' (Artistotle, 1934, 1103a26–1103b2). To this it should be added that skills are not unchangeable, even though they are more stable than the particular instances of their being performed. There is always the possibility that they will improve or degenerate.

In the language of today – and with a greater possibility for empirical measurement – we can say that skills are combinations of automaticity and awareness (i.e. conscious monitoring and possible correction in the performance of the task). There are varying degrees of automatising and conscious monitoring. The combination of these two ways of performing tasks will vary according to the type of task being performed, the purpose of the task, etc. Developing a skill entails developing an automatisation, the ability to consciously monitor one's performance, and the ability to combine these in productive ways.

We can have a great deal of knowledge about the physical laws pertaining to how bodies float on water but still not be able to swim. Aristotle's dictum on practice is valid here. Bicycling is another skill that is developed through practice. A high degree of automatisation is necessary. If you think too much about the whys and hows of balancing on two wheels, you will fall. But if you bicycle too much on autopilot, you will not be able to tackle unexpected situations in a flexible manner. We cannot say, however, that a skill is awareness + automaticity. Rather, it is the most situationally appropriate combination thereof. These two aspects form a unified whole – just as mind and body are a unified whole. A tightrope-walker, for example, is not a person who in addition to performing certain movements on a tight-rope *also* has a certain awareness of these actions. As mentioned, both the 'inner' (mental) and the 'outer' (physical) aspects of a skill are part of the definition of that skill. Therefore, when cognitive psychology puts much weight on identifying and performing 'sub-skills', this may create more problems than it solves. From a logical point of view it may be clarifying to split reading into its smallest, atomary units. From a psychological and educational point of view, by contrast, it may be extremely challenging. Some people will find the subject too abstract. Others will find it difficult to shift in a natural way between parts and the whole – as it were, between the trees and the wood.

It is important to note that the relationship among sub-skills is *definitory*, that is, logical and not empirical. We can illustrate this with the following example: (a) a judge is a person who, on behalf of the state and in accordance with the law, pronounces verdicts in court cases; and (b) there are a number of laws and rules that *define* what tasks this entails in practice. We can say that (a) is equivalent to the skill, while (b) is equivalent to sub-skills. Both (a) and (b) are parts of the *definition* of 'judge'. The question of how the judge *ought to*, say, treat the prosecutor and the defence counsel cannot be answered empirically, by looking at how judges actually perform. The answer must be found in the definitions and rules regulating the judge's activities. Similarly, it is a commonplace to *define* 'reading' as a skill which includes sub-skills such as comprehension and phonological analysis and synthesis. If we lay down categorical definitions of concepts such as 'reading' or 'dyslexia', we thereby exclude them from empirical research and insulate them from change. In my opinion, all definitions must be perceived and treated as hypotheses in need of adjustment as and when empirical research so requires (cf. Tønnessen, 1997a).

In addition to reading, important examples of skills are intelligence and language skills. Often skills are conceived of and referred to as if they were delimited and localised entities (e.g., in Jerry Fodor's modular theory of mind: Fodor, 1983). Hypostatising or substantiating in this manner is misleading. Just as the fragility of a glass surface is both nowhere to be found in the glass itself and everywhere in it, we cannot localise skills. Even though you are in Norway, it makes no sense to conceive of your reading ability as also being in Norway …

However, we can describe the conditions *necessary* for reading, such as awareness, certain linguistic skills, vision, etc.

We need to be clear about the difference between 'skill' and the 'performance' or actualisation of a skill. Even though a skill changes over time, it is still more stable than the actualisations of it. This is important to take into consideration when diagnosing and treating reading disabilities. Actual instances of reading are highly influenced by motivation, concentration, the reading situation and the like. To the extent that a person's reading difficulties are due to such circumstances, efforts should be made to improve them. Doing so will usually be easier than trying to improve the skill itself.

How do we learn skills?

The expression 'tacit knowledge' is often associated with Michael Polanyi (1973). He expressed his basic point in the sentence: 'We know more than we can tell.' We see this clearly in practical skills such as swimming, bicycling and the like. We are not able to acquire these skills through reading or hearing about them, and we cannot explain them fully to another person with words alone. This is not because of any lack of verbal ability; it is because these skills are not about 'knowledge' in the usual sense (cf. Wittgenstein, 1922, 4.1212: 'What *can* be shown, *cannot* be said'). They are 'knowing how', not 'knowing that'. Another term for 'knowing how' is 'procedural knowledge' – or 'tacit knowledge'. Procedural or tacit knowledge is not about following rules. It is more apt to say that the activity in question is *in accordance with* rules, not that the person exhibiting the skill is *following* rules intentionally and fully consciously. Often we can only claim that there is a *regularity or pattern* in the activity.

Even though we cannot describe precisely the regularity or patterns in a complex activity (such as swimming or riding a bicycle), our consciousness can nonetheless be trained to monitor these activities and take over control of them in some circumstances. Control and correction such as this makes the difference between, say, a good and a poor pianist. This is typical of all kinds of skills.

Even though skills cannot be learned through theoretical teaching alone, not all such teaching is worthless. Learning through examples – seeing the behaviour modelled – is also important. Skills are primarily acquired through 'implicit learning' and practice (Reber, 1993).

Potentiality and language

Like other skills, language skill is a kind of potentiality. For example, when we are asleep, our entire language skill exists only as a potentiality. When we are awake, we may use parts of it while other parts exist only as potentialities. Moreover, language is primarily a skill, not a system as claimed by Chomsky (1957, 2006) and others. Language can only be studied through linguistic acts – as realisations of language skills. By means of empirical methods we may find regularities and patterns in language performance at various times and places. We cannot, however, use the term 'system' in the same meaning as it has in relation to, say, carefully constructed philosophical systems. Regularities and patterns in language performance are subject to continuous change. Grammar as a scientific discipline consists of empirically based generalisations with limited scope. Researchers, authors, teachers and others may use those generalisations to formulate normative recommendations about how to use language in order to obtain specific goals when it comes to expressing thoughts and feelings, but it must be questioned to what extent such recommendations can be seen as empirically based.

The concept of 'potentiality' is also necessary in defining *linguistic meaning*. Plato claimed that concepts or ideas were located in an unchanging 'realm of ideas'. According to this way of thinking, we label a person a 'human' because he or she exhibits characteristics that are in accord with the unchanging definition. During the Middle Ages this notion of 'conceptual realism' was criticised by the 'nominalists', who claimed that only particular instances existed. Both ways of looking at things reduce potentiality to actuality – to either abstract *ideas* or concrete spoken or written *words*.

An alternative solution is to look at words as *variables*. In mathematics, a variable is something that has a value within a certain range. For example, we can say that x is a variable within the *range* of whole numbers from 5 to 11. The seven numbers 5, 6, 7, 8, 9, 10 and 11 then form a set. At any one time, x can have only one of these values (thus, in a sense, the nominalists are correct). But it must be added that x can *potentially* have any of the seven values. By adding the notion of 'potentiality' we assume a middle stance between the conceptual realists and the nominalists. We can illustrate this point by using the word 'man' as an example. Among the potential meanings of this word we find: (a) 'an adult male human being', (b) 'a human being of either sex', (c) 'the human race' and (d) 'a husband'. The word potentially has all these – and other – meanings, but it has only one meaning at a time. It should also be added that grammatical moods are one part of the potentials of meaning. The word 'help' may for example be used in an indicative mood ('Paul needs help.'), in an imperative mood ('Help!') or as a question ('Does Paul need help?'). The possible meanings (and moods) taken together delimit the range of the word – just like a given set of numbers delimits the possible values of a variable. Contexts, situations, persons, etc., determine which of the potential meanings is actualised.

Empirical studies are necessary to delimit these fields of meaning. Meaning is a potential that signs (codes, symbols, etc.) 'have'. How this potential is realised depends on the person, intention, situation, etc. Empirical investigation must be based on physical reactions elicited by linguistic acts, and on interpretations of those reactions. The goal of empirical investigations is to obtain descriptions, definitions, explanations and understanding. As mentioned above, meaning involves both 'outer' and 'inner' aspects. Based on investigations of reactions we may formulate hypotheses of meaning, although we will never attain exhaustive and unchangeable definitions. There are usually several sets of possible realisations of potentials for meaning. These, however, are not as clearly defined as in mathematics. They are more like magnetic fields, where at the centre we find the most common meanings. A field of possible meanings can also change over time and place. In studies of the type referred to here it is not useful to draw sharp lines between semantics, pragmatics and hermeneutics. A certain meaning cannot be localised to a certain element in the overall linguistic code or string of signs, nor to the non-linguistic context. Attempting to localise exactly where the meaning arises in, say, a poem or other 'message' is as impossible as localising where the fragility of a glass surface 'is': it is everywhere and nowhere.

READING SKILL

INTRODUCTION

In this chapter, we will describe and explain what it means that reading is – or is based on – a *skill*. We will use the overall (singular) term 'reading', and we will argue that this can be seen as a single skill. While it is perfectly possible to break reading down into several sub-skills, the main objective of this chapter is to show that, like any other skill, it constitutes a combination of automaticity and awareness. This means that the concept of 'skill' combines key ideas of both behaviourism and cognitivism – and thus also of connectionism.

We distinguish between reading skill as such and the performance of that skill. A person's performance of a skill may vary because of situational and motivational factors while the skill itself is more stable. A further point to be kept in mind is that (literate) people, even when they are not reading, retain their reading skill as a potential in the same way as, say, intelligence is still there as a potential when someone is asleep.

Against the backdrop of our distinction between a skill and its performance, it may be useful to ask what the goal of reading research is. Is it to investigate reading behaviour? If so, any findings are likely to shed light on individual differences in reading pace and reading mistakes. However, the typical purpose of reading tests, as reflected both in their design and in their administration, is rather to obtain a picture of the underlying reading skill (and this is true of IQ tests as well: like reading tests, they aim to investigate the abilities enabling us to act in certain ways). Reading has traditionally been broken down into decoding and comprehension. In our view, these two parts can be brought together in a special way by hermeneutics, through the concept of 'interpretation'.

A review of the research literature on reading and reading difficulties shows that 'skills' and 'abilities' are rarely mentioned while 'processes' and 'models' are more frequent concepts, used to describe the tasks that must be solved in order to go from script to meaning. Such descriptions show what a reader must be able to do – they do not primarily concern knowledge, but rather skills. Sometimes those tasks will be performed well, meaning that the person will read well. On other occasions the tasks will be solved less well, and so reading performance will be less good. Reading skill, however, may remain the same regardless of such variation.

Underpinning this chapter is a conviction that having an insight into the basic questions and their answers will strongly influence the choices teachers make in their professional practice. In a certain sense, there is nothing as practical as a good theory. Those who have not thought deeply about the fundamental issues will fall easy prey to new trends coming into fashion.

The literature in the field of reading research is extensive, meaning that writing a short chapter requires making big choices. Below, we will first briefly present a small selection of theories and approaches that we see as central to the history of reading research. They all have something to say both about the sub-tasks of reading and about how those can be carried out. Then we will present a number of processes that have been central to large parts of reading research. Finally, we will try to bring together the above in order to show how various elements may supplement each other in a fruitful understanding of reading skill.

THEORIES AND APPROACHES IN READING RESEARCH

This section will give brief characterisations of the schools of psychology that we consider to have been the most central to the study of reading: behaviourism, cognitivism and connectionism. However, the first sub-section deals not with a school of psychology as such, but rather with an approach to research – the visual one, which originally attracted the strongest interest in reading research. This involves both the eye, sensing, perception and memory, meaning that medical and psychological issues alike are relevant in this context.

The main focus below will be on ideas of special importance to views on reading and the investigation of reading. As we will see, this applies in particular to automaticity, awareness and interpretation.

The visual approach

The first studies of reading and reading difficulties placed their main focus on the visual: eye movements, visual sensing and visual perception as well as visual memory. The latter can be broken down into iconic memory, which is a very brief gathering of impulses immediately after sensory impressions reach the eyes; short-term memory, to which the impressions then proceed; working memory, where they can subsequently be more actively processed; and finally long-term memory, where they can be stored.

Where to draw the line between sensing and perception is controversial, but at least iconic and short-term memory are often counted as part of the sensing system. Processing in working memory, however, is part of perception and involves interpreting sensory impressions. This processing is based not only on the impressions as such, but also depends on long-term memory and on recognition or cognition: to interpret the word 'sun', a person must both recognise the image (spelling) of the word using long-term memory and think a few thoughts about what the sun is like. In the earliest studies of reading difficulties, researchers assumed that the main problems of dyslectics related to visual sensing and perception (this explains why 'word blindness' was a common term). Later on, the position of the eyes (e.g. the presence of a squint) and their movement were also identified as possible causes of reading difficulties (Miles & Miles, 2001).

Until about 1960, reading research primarily concerned itself with the eye-movement patterns of readers in general and dyslectics in particular. The reason for this may well be that eye movements lend themselves to more exact measurement than do sensing and perception. The characteristic features of eye movements during reading are jumping movements often referred to as 'saccades'. These occur between 'fixations'. During a fixation, which is when information is primarily gathered, the eyes stay focused for 200–500 milliseconds. Then there is a saccade to a point about ten letters further on in the direction of reading. The saccade lasts for 20–50 milliseconds, during which time only a minimum of information is taken in. In the event of problems, the reader will carry out 'regressions' by jumping backwards in the text to pick up the thread again. Ever-more sophisticated instruments and measuring methods show considerable variation in eye-movement patterns during reading (Rayner & Pollatsek, 1989).

Even though reading research from the 1960s onwards has paid less attention to visual matters, this approach has been taken forward, in particular through neurological studies showing that it is possible to distinguish between a parvocellular system and a magnocellular one. The parvocellular system, which from an evolutionary perspective is considered to be a younger, more 'modern' component of human physiology than the magnocellular one, is primarily concentrated in the pupils and is used to focus on details when the eye is at rest, meaning that it is used above all during fixations. The magnocellular system is involved in peripheral vision, which is coarser and yields larger units, and is also able to record movement. It is responsible for informing a person when to end a fixation and whether there is a need to make a regression in order to 'get back on track'. In addition, it provides information enabling the length of the next saccade to be determined. It is assumed that the problems of dyslexics are located mainly in the magnocellular system (Stein, 2001).

Behaviourism

From the 1930s to the 1960s, various strands of behaviourism dominated both psychology in general and the psychology of reading and reading instruction in particular. Behaviourism is a heterogeneous school of psychology; for our present purposes, we would like to emphasise the following tenets as characteristic: (a) psychology should be based only on that which is externally observable; (b) people learn by making associations; (c) associations are reinforced by repetition; (d) automatised, rapid and energy-saving responses are a consequence of this; and (e) emotions and instincts or needs explain motivation and cause people to respond to reward and punishment (Leahey, 2001). In other words, the psychological driving forces are irrational. We will see later on that it is less clear what the driving forces are in cognitive psychology, which places its main focus on the rational. It should be noted that behaviourism, unlike parts of cognitive psychology, sees learning how to read not as a special case, but as based on general principles of learning (Baum, 2005). Omaggio (1993) describes the psychology of reading of 1950s behaviourism as emphasising 'habit formation, brought about by

57

the repeated association of a stimulus with a response' (p. 45). Language was seen as a 'response system that humans acquire through automatic conditioning processes [...] some patterns of language are reinforced (rewarded) and others are not [...] only those patterns reinforced by the community of language users will persist' (p. 46). A great deal of importance was attributed to language habits, repetition and drilling.

Behaviourists used various methods and elements in reading instruction, but a central position progressively came to be occupied by Phonics (a teaching method placing special emphasis on awareness of language sounds; cf. the chapter on reading instruction in this book). Samuels and Kamil (1984) claim that 'little attempt was made to explain what went on within the recesses of the mind that allowed the human to make sense of the printed page' (p. 25). Representatives of cognitive psychology contend that Phonics was used differently in their circles, but – as we will see – that school also draws strongly on association and automatisation (Samuels & Kamil, 1984).

According to Baum (2005), behaviourism evolved and became more diverse after J.B. Watson formulated its most important basic principles in the 1920s. We will not go into historical details here, but a quotation from Watson (1930) of relevance to teaching may be an appropriate starting point:

> Give me a dozen healthy infants, well-formed, and my own specified world to bring them up in and I'll guarantee to take any one at random and train him to become any type of specialist I might select – doctor, lawyer, artist, merchant-chief and, yes, even beggar-man and thief, regardless of his talents, penchants, tendencies, abilities, vocations, and race of his ancestors. (p. 82)

This statement may be intentionally drastic, but even so it is typical that the student is seen as highly passive, and the teacher as correspondingly active, in the context of education and instruction. Teaching becomes superficial and mechanical. The children are exposed to specific stimuli intended to elicit specific responses. In this respect, Watson's student B.F. Skinner was more open-minded. He assigned greater importance to the children's power of initiative and to their spontaneity, emphasising that desirable actions should be rewarded (reinforced) to increase the likelihood that they will be repeated. Further, Skinner took a negative view of punishment, but the implications of this are open to discussion. If criticism and the correction of mistakes are perceived as punishment and thus discouraged, learning by failing will not be very effective, and as the philosopher of science Karl Popper has shown, falsification – or trial and error – is the most effective method in human problem-solving and learning (Popper, 1959). As we will see later, the cognitive psychologist Kenneth S. Goodman considered that this insight should underpin reading instruction.

Cognitivism

The boundary between behaviourism and cognitive psychology can be identified by reference to Ausubel (1968), a cognitive psychologist who emphasised the difference between meaningful learning and rote learning. However, the various strands of cognitive psychology place more or less weight on meaning – some of them focus more on concepts such as 'awareness' and 'metacognition' (thinking about thinking).

Yetta M. Goodman and Kenneth S. Goodman are among those who assign great importance to meaning, stressing that readers create meaning in their encounters with texts (while other cognitivists in reading research play this position down or disagree with it). For example, Goodman and Goodman (1994) assert the following:

> Reading is not simply knowing sounds, words, sentences, and the abstract parts of language that can be studied by linguists. Reading, like listening, consists of processing language and constructing meaning. The reader brings a great deal of information to this complex and active process. […] As readers make use of their knowledge of all the language cues, they predict, make inferences, select significant features, confirm, and constantly work toward constructing a meaningful text. Not only are they constructing meaning. They are constructing themselves as readers. (pp. 112–115).

In this connection, Liberman, Shankweiler and Liberman (1989) stress, among other things, that there is an essential difference between written language and spoken language in that proper application of the alphabetic principle requires awareness of the internal phonological structure of words represented using the alphabet, and that – unfortunately for emerging readers and writers – such awareness is not an automatic consequence of speaking a language. For this reason, Phonics and phonemic awareness have been at the centre of much cognitivist reading research. Starting from a meaning-focused variety of cognitivism, Goodman and Goodman (1994) claim that Phonics should not be taught, because children 'can discover letter-sound regularities from experiencing actual print and doing real writing' (p. 22). This may be an extreme position, but we will see later on that both implicit learning and the ability to notice (as opposed to just seeing) are things that must be kept in mind when it comes to children's reading and their acquisition of reading skill. Indeed, Goodman and Goodman (1994) presuppose, in several places, that reading consists primarily of associating entire words with meaning. Because of the essential role of association, this can be claimed to be an element of behaviourism

Cognitivists who have criticised the Goodmans and those like-minded have started from dual-route (or two-channel) models. According to Seymour (1986), dual-route models are based on the claim that 'the interpretation of an array of letters typically involves the co-operation of two functionally distinct processes: a lexical process, by which the pronunciation of known words may be directly "looked up" or addressed, and a non-lexical process which makes use of a knowledge of letter-sound associations to assemble a conventionally acceptable pronunciation' (p. 5). Since one of those routes corresponds to the Goodmans' direct route from meaning to pronunciation, we are dealing with association here as well. The other route requires words to be broken down into letters (graphemes), which must then first of all be recognised or identified. This, too, is a matter of association. To avoid, say, mistaking the letters J and L for each other, a reader must have established, by means of a large number of repetitions, clear representations of the differences between them. Then, once the graphemes have been identified, they must be associated with language sounds (phonemes). After that, the phonemes are combined into a sound package, which is associated with a meaning. Even when this procedure is used, then, behaviourist laws of association clearly play an absolutely central role.

As mentioned, association is closely linked to repetition, automatisation and rapid, energy-saving responses. The cognitive element primarily consists in the analysis of a written image and the synthesis of phonemes. The analysis of the written image relates above all to visual sensing and perception. As we have seen, these are closely related. Some might assert that sensing is non-cognitive, while it is commonly claimed that perception is cognitive because interpretation is an important component of it. When phonemes are to be combined into a sound package, there is a need for memory. Some will say this is short-term memory, others will contend that working memory is the best term. Both of these are central to cognitive psychology.

Unlike behaviourism, the cognitive school does not restrict itself to the externally observable. Instead, the internal – often referred to as mental processes – is the main object of interest. As already mentioned, this creates room for aspects such as meaning, awareness and metacognition. However, it is striking that cognitivists have been more concerned with structures and models than with processes and internal driving forces such as emotions and needs. Part of the reason for this may be that cognitivists have drawn inspiration from the linguist Noam Chomsky and from computer technology (particularly artificial intelligence or AI) (Leahey, 2001). As a rule, no explicit emphasis is placed on introspection (subjective observation of one's inner life), but it is otherwise open to discussion what type of empirical data makes up the foundation of this school. Its reading models, which often constitute detailed presentations of the dual-route model, show the various sub-tasks that reading can be assumed to consist of. These models can be compared to anatomical models of the human skeleton and inner organs: they provide a picture of the structure, but not of the driving forces explaining life. On this point, cognitivism differs from behaviourism, which shows how emotions and needs make people react to reward and punishment, and also explains variation in motivation. Such irrational factors are difficult to accommodate even in a very broad concept of cognition.

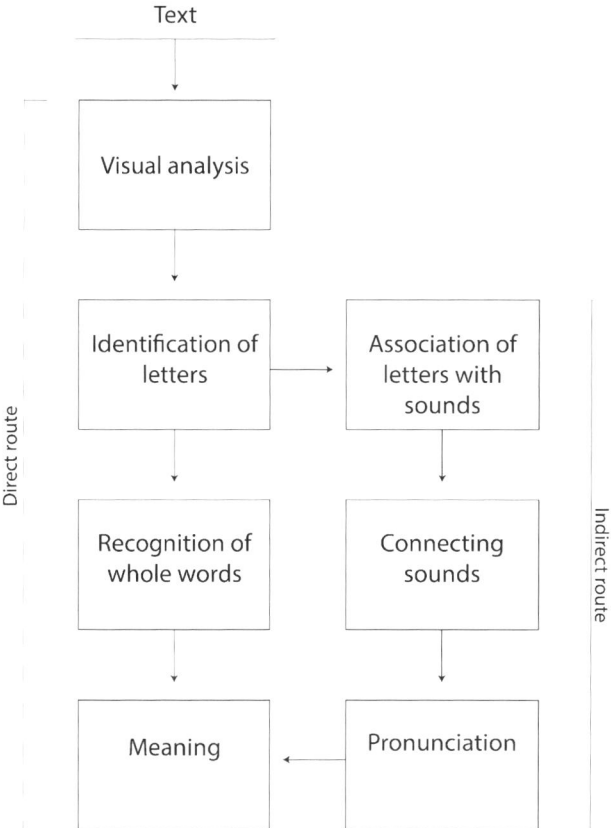

Figure 1. A cognitivist model of reading

As mentioned, the cognitive models show how reading can be broken down into sub-tasks. This is particularly useful in the diagnosing of reading difficulties: the more accurately the problems can be localised, the more specific interventions it will be possible to make. The models thus show where there are problems, but they do not show why or how the problems have arisen. When it comes to both the development of skills and limitations to skills, we are of the opinion that connectionism can give better answers than cognitive psychology.

Connectionism

Some historical overviews treat connectionism together with cognitivism. In our opinion, however, connectionism has more in common with behaviourism in that its main focus is on the workings of nerve cells. Like in behaviourism, automatisation is a key concept. However, connectionism places more emphasis on the idea that nerve cells may be more or less 'fired up'. This makes it possible to explain not only occasional sub-optimal performance of tasks but also progressive acquisition and progressive loss of knowledge and skills. Like behaviourism, connectionism is better than cognitivism at explaining individual differences.

Unlike behaviourism, connectionism does not restrict itself to the externally observable. But unlike cognitivism, it still refuses to use 'mentalist' language such as 'inner representations' and 'ideas'. As a result, concepts such as 'meaning' and 'representation' are rare in connectionist writings. Nor does connectionism assume the existence of such clearly delimited abilities or modules as are often found in cognitivism (cf. Fodor, 1983). Further, while cognitivism assumes a clear distinction between the rational and the irrational and also often distinguishes more or less clearly between the psychological and the physical, connectionism asserts that such distinctions cannot be made. This avoids many of the problems that arise in cognitivism. However, critics consider this to be a way for connectionism to disregard individual problems. For example, it can be objected on good grounds that it is difficult to find a place for meaning in connectionist thought, even though connectionist models of reading always include a 'semantic processor' (Rogers & McClelland, 2004). A further potential objection is that connectionism has little place for the control function which is included in the cognitivist framework in the form of awareness or conscious monitoring and steering. On this last point, though, connectionists would assert that the nervous system has an inherent tendency to find balance or harmony. Problems and tensions are resolved in a way that resembles how this is done in a cybernetic system, with feedback from one part of the system influencing the remainder. When it comes to learning, this actually resembles Jean Piaget's theory of assimilation and accommodation (Piaget, 1966).

Like cognitivism, connectionism often uses models showing activities on the internal level. However, connectionist models are usually less detailed than cognitivist ones. Further, while cognitivism typically assumes that the sub-tasks included in a model are carried out in a specific order and one at a time, connectionism claims that many processes are going on simultaneously or in parallel (this is why connectionism is occasionally referred to as 'parallel distributed processing' or PDP). In addition, connectionism has an interesting theory about 'emergence', according to which there occasionally arise cascades of reactions whose result is more than the sum of the inputs. This can be compared to the concept of 'insight' in gestalt psychology, where there are sudden leaps in comprehension. As we will see later on, something similar can also be found in the distinction between seeing and noticing. Children spelling or sounding their way through a word often experience the type of sudden revelations sometimes referred to as 'Aha! moments'. For example, the word 'summer' may be read out as /s/-/ʌ/- /m/-/m/-/ə/-/r/. Then suddenly everything falls into place and the child realises the correct meaning. But if, say, lexical stress is misplaced or the process is too slow, a child may not discover what the corresponding spoken word is.

Connectionism has turned out to be a good fit with the workings of the nervous system. This school of psychology has also managed to develop software that very successfully simulates the consequences of learning and of damage to the nervous system. Simulations of, for example, how children learn the past-tense forms of English irregular verbs have shown that these ideas are very fruitful and that the simulations imitate reality well (cf. Rumelhart & McClelland, 1986).

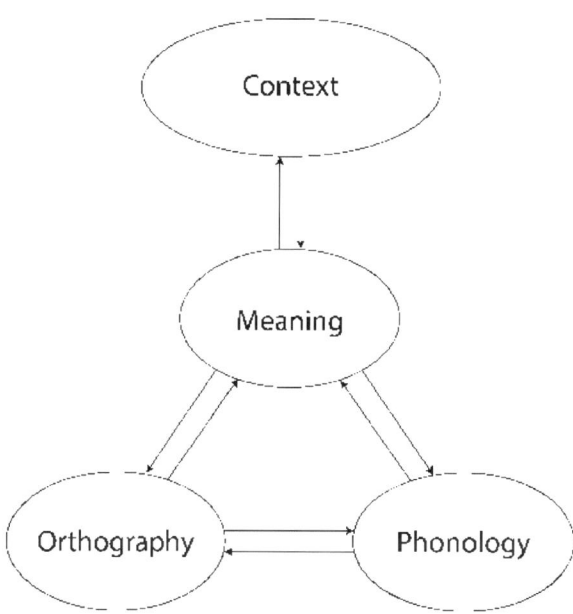

Figure 2. A connectionist model of reading (cf. Seidenberg & McClelland, 1989)

PROCESSES

It is open to discussion whether 'process' is the most appropriate term to describe what happens when people read, to encompass the methods they use to solve the tasks or problems that reading confronts them with. In fact, this word may evoke associations to chemistry and chemical reactions (sequences of events governed by immutable laws). Since reading is largely automatised, this may easily lead to the impression that a chain reaction is triggered when the text meets the eye, eventually making the reader find meaning in the text. In reality, however, what happens is that a series of tasks and problems are solved. To understand what reading is, it is necessary to know what those tasks and problems consist in and how people go about solving them.

In the following discussion, we will refer to three overall methods or approaches, commonly called the bottom-up approach, the top-down approach and the interactive approach, which are used during reading in different contexts and to a varying extent. We will use these established terms even though we find the first two of them somewhat misleading. What we dislike about them is that they are figurative expressions presupposing that reading can be compared to the placing of building-blocks on top of each other. First and most obviously, this is because these expressions evoke a sequence from the point when the written image reaches the eye to the point when the reader identifies a pronunciation and a meaning. However, there is probably also often an underlying idea that the first or bottom blocks are simpler or less complicated than the top ones. This is why it is more common to talk about automatisation in relation to the bottom blocks. In our opinion, first, both automatisation and awareness are needed at all levels; and, second – as we will show later – it is more appropriate to talk in terms of the relationship between the whole and its parts than in terms of that between the top and the bottom.

Bottom-up approach

Opinions differ as regards how many building-blocks there are between the bottom and the top. We will not discuss this issue in detail here, only mention a few main blocks that are usually included in descriptions.

Reading theory generally distinguishes between graphemes and phonemes. These concepts exhibit some variation as regards their use and content, but generally speaking phonemes are language sounds used to express meaning. The word 'sun' thus contains three phonemes. A grapheme is a graphical representation of a phoneme. Basically, this means that there is one grapheme (or letter) corresponding to each phoneme. Such correspondences are of course rarely perfect – one grapheme may represent several phonemes and a phoneme may be represented by several graphemes.

The manifestations of graphemes and phonemes encountered in real life are not uniform. Since there are handwritten and printed versions of individual graphemes, in various fonts, in bold and italic type, upper- and lower-case letters, etc., the identification of graphemes must be based on both sensing, perception and memory. Identification thus presupposes interpretation, and this is true of phonemes as well. For example, the realisation of the phoneme corresponding to the <a> grapheme will have a slightly different ring to it depending on who is speaking. This variation is associated, among other things, with gender, age and dialect. The phoneme has been compared to an atom, which consists of a nucleus surrounded by a 'cloud' of electrons: the nucleus represents the common features of the phoneme while the cloud represents this variation in its pronunciation.

Despite this need for interpretation, however, there is a large extent of automatisation in the identification of graphemes and phonemes. On the other hand, as we will discuss in greater detail later, what is happening automatically must be 'monitored' so that any problems that arise may be solved and any mistakes may be corrected.

When the written image has been broken down into graphemes, each grapheme is associated with a phoneme. These phonemes are then brought together to form a pronunciation. If the word is long, or if the phonemes are brought together too slowly, it may be that some sounds escape from memory. For example, some of the first sounds in 'summertime' may be forgotten, and then there is no way to find out to which of the words of spoken language the sound package corresponds. Now, if the model involves such a sound package being compared with words of spoken language, there must be some form of external or internal pronunciation. Except in the case of reading aloud, however, the nature of this pronunciation is a controversial issue: is it sub-vocal (i.e. involving movements of the vocal chords that do not produce any audible sounds), or is it entirely mental?

Analysis and synthesis here involve a complicated combination of the whole and its parts. What is required, in a sense, is the ability to tell the trees from the forest. A person with normal vision will see all words and their component parts, but may not necessarily notice all of the relevant details, perhaps focusing instead on too large a number of small details or on too small a number of large ones.

Cognitive psychology has devoted a great deal of attention to models such as the dual-route one, which consists of a direct route and an indirect one. Here, two things should be noted. First, it is a well-known fact that good readers really do see words as wholes and associate them with meaning. Second, there is a consensus that unfamiliar words must be broken down into graphemes, which are then associated with phonemes. As we will see later on, the distinction between the direct route and the indirect one largely corresponds to our distinction between automaticity and awareness. However, it should be added that the indirect route requires both automaticity and awareness. This is because it presupposes that the association between grapheme and phoneme has been automatised. If a reader recognises parts of a word, such as a few syllables or morphemes, there will not just be a need for association between phonemes and graphemes, but also for association between larger units. This could be claimed to represent an additional route, meaning that there are more than two. However, in our opinion the two-way distinction is appropriate given that the indirect route requires analysis and synthesis – to a greater or lesser extent – while the direct one does not. The phonemes must be brought together to form wholes, which must be compared with words of spoken language.

This two-way idea has been known and used since the beginnings of reading research, but it was not formally made into a dual-route model until the arrival of cognitivism. It is debatable who was the first to represent this idea graphically, but Morton (1968) was at least one of the first to do so. The first route, leading from whole words to meaning and/or pronunciation, can be fully explained by the laws of association of behaviourism. The second, indirect, route is also largely based on those laws, namely as regards the connection between graphemes and phonemes. What it requires in addition to those laws is analysis and synthesis, tasks primarily based on sensing, perception and memory. Perception and memory would be seen by most people as cognitive tasks, but even so many would also claim that behaviourism can explain memory in terms of associations.

When it comes to the analysis of written images, there is a need for visual skills. Not only must the visual organs and the sensing system function properly, but there is also a requirement for perception, which really is interpretation: to make sense of difficult handwriting, for example, the relevant details must be identified. Those details must always be interpreted in the light of larger wholes, but the size of the wholes chosen in this context is an open question. In other words, there are no limits specifying what the smallest or largest units are. To this should be added that memory must also be used to determine, say, whether a letter is a J or an L.

The synthesis of language sounds requires auditory and phonological skills. Whether phonological skills can be reduced to auditory skills is a controversial question. In our view, auditory skills are a prerequisite for phonological ones. Phonology is about sounds, but primarily about distinguishing language sounds from other sounds and distinguishing between different language sounds. In other words, it is largely a question of identification and categorisation. Synthesis requires, first, that an increasing number of phonemes are maintained in working memory – for example, first /s/, then /ʌ/ and finally /n/. Further, it is important to bring these together into a whole: 'sun'. While what matters in analysis is identifying the trees, the key to synthesis is identifying the forest. The latter task consists in comparing the whole arrived at with a word of spoken language located in memory. At first glance this may seem a simple task, but most people will have noticed that early beginning readers may run into problems in this context. For example, if a child devotes too much time to each of the sounds of the word 'sun' or places the stress incorrectly, he or she will have difficulty realising that this sound package corresponds to a familiar word in spoken language.

In reading-instruction theory, the Phonics tradition (see the chapter on reading instruction in this book for further explanation) is the one that has placed the most emphasis on the bottom-up approach. Both behaviourism and large parts of cognitive psychology have been part of the Phonics tradition, based on the argument that this approach is necessary to read unfamiliar words. The Whole Language (or Whole Word) tradition (again, see the chapter on reading instruction in this book for more details) represents the other extreme of reading-instruction theory yet also belongs to the cognitive school of psychology. Its advocates do accept that the indirect route can be helpful to solve some problems, but also claim that motivation and meaning can be lost if excessive emphasis is placed on that method. In addition, they see a risk that children will become too preoccupied with the trees and lose sight of the forest.

Top-down approach

When faced with entirely new phenomena, people do not normally start with the smallest details. Let us take as an example how scholars have gone about understanding the Voynich manuscript, described as 'the world's most mysterious manuscript' (Brumbaugh, 1977). They first tried to form an overall impression of the whole: When was the manuscript written? By whom? For whom? Why? What is the main point? While not arriving at any certain and clear answers to these questions, scholars made guesses, assumptions and hypotheses that were more or less well-founded, primarily using their imagination and their creativity. Only then did they try to make sense of the details of the manuscript in the light of these overall considerations. This is a typical example of the top-down approach. The more unfamiliar and unknown a phenomenon is, the more overall in nature the approach taken to it will be. In the case of reading, neither the written image nor the meaning is likely to be as unknown as in the case of the Voynich manuscript, which is why there is rarely a need to take such an overall approach and place such emphasis on it.

As mentioned above, the Whole Language school of reading instruction represents a top-down view of the reading process. This school belongs to cognitivism, which focuses mainly on the meaning-related aspect of reading. If experienced readers encounter an unfamiliar word, they will follow the indirect route, with analysis and synthesis, as described above. However, if the word is entirely unfamiliar in terms of both meaning, spelling and pronunciation, this route will not be very helpful. If, say, the word is from a language completely unfamiliar to the reader, he or she will end up with a sound package but will not know how to pronounce it nor what it means. Then the word must be looked up on the internet or in a dictionary. This requires knowledge and skills: being able to key in the letters in correct order in a search box or knowing how the letters of a word can be used to find it in a dictionary. And if such a search is successful, it will often turn out that the word has several potential meanings. Then it is necessary to study the context in which the word is used in order to find the most likely or appropriate meaning.

Such problems potentially caused by entirely unknown words are evidence that the bottom-up approach is not always effective. Kenneth S. Goodman (Goodman, 1967), when referring to reading as a 'guessing game', may have been out to provoke by his choice of words, but still it is often the case that readers are able to make good assumptions about the meaning of unfamiliar words based on their context – and sometimes such assumptions may even be more helpful than dictionary entries.

Interactive approach

When it comes to the interactive approach, the most influential school of psychology may be connectionism. This approach, first, does not involve sequential processes where one task is completed before the next one is begun but allows for parallel or simultaneous processes. Second, this approach also allows for interaction among all sub-processes.

In addition, there is no clear-cut distinction between 'top' and 'bottom', as can be seen from the connectionist David E. Rumelhart's choice of terminology:

> I use the term perception rather freely here. In general, it is my opinion that the distinction between the perceptual and conceptual aspects of reading is not that useful. As I will suggest later, there appears to be a continuity between what has been called perception and what has been called comprehension. My use of the term perception in the present context is simply the use of the one term to cover the entire process. (Rumelhart in Ruddell, Ruddell, & Singer, 1994, note on p. 893)

As is clear from the model of Seidenberg and McClelland (1989) presented above, these connectionists presuppose an interaction between various 'processors': a context processor, a meaning (or semantic) processor, an orthographic processor and a phonological processor. To this could be added sensing and perception, which are closely associated with comprehension and cognition in the above quotation from Rumelhart.

Marilyn Jager Adams, who wrote one of the most influential books – *Beginning to Read* – about reading and reading instruction, has the following to say about the connectionist way of thinking:

> The power of these models derives from the fact that they are neither top-down nor bottom-up in nature. Instead, all relevant processes they include are simultaneously active and interactive; all simultaneously issue and accommodate information to and from one another. The key to these models, in other words, is not the dominance of one set of processes over the others, but the coordination and cooperation of all as shaped by the reader's own prior knowledge and experience. (Adams in Ruddell, Ruddell, & Singer, 1994, p. 843)

READING SKILL

As initially mentioned, we intend to conclude this chapter by trying to bring together some of the threads of the discussion in order to investigate what it means that reading is a skill.

Let us first examine the claim that reading is a skill similarly to, say, intelligence. When people are asleep and not using their intelligence, it is still there as a potential to solve problems and perform other tasks. The same applies to reading. We thus cannot agree with behaviourism, which restricts reading to external observable reading behaviour or to performance on reading tests. If reading skill is to be measured, it is of course important to have access to good tests that measure this skill or potential as accurately as possible. This means that those tests should have high validity and reliability. In this context, the difference between reading skill as such and its performance is important. For example, if a student is having difficulties showing his or her true potential because of poor concentration or nervousness, it is important to take measures to remedy these factors. By contrast, if the actual skill or potential is inadequate, there is a need to take much more far-reaching action.

There is also, as mentioned to begin with, a need to distinguish between knowledge and skills. Typical examples of knowledge are facts gathered in memory relating to, say, geographical names or years that are important in history. Typical examples of skills include swimming and riding a bicycle. It is not unusual for knowledge and skills to be interwoven. A person who speaks a foreign language can be said to possess a skill, but that skill also consists in knowledge about the pronunciation and meaning of words in that language. By emphasising that reading is a skill, we do thus not exclude that reading may also require knowledge, above all knowledge about spelling.

What, then, characterises the good performance of a skill? The most important thing is to find an optimal combination of automaticity and awareness. The concept of automaticity comes from the behaviourist tradition, which led to an excessive preoccupation with automatisation in reading instruction, making reading mechanical and superficial. The concept of awareness comes from the cognitivist tradition, which has focused too much on metacognition and on knowledge of rules. Both behaviourism and cognitivism represent important insights that must be taken into account in order to understand what reading is and how this skill can best be acquired. In our opinion, connectionism has combined these two schools of psychology in a way which is very fruitful to reading research and reading instruction. Our terminology, however, differs slightly from that used by connectionism.

What do we mean by an optimal combination of automaticity and awareness? What is crucial is that the respective weight allocated to these must be adapted to the circumstances. Let us take a concrete example from a field other than reading. A person riding a bicycle who relies completely on the 'autopilot' may end up in trouble. But so may a person who thinks too much about what he or she is doing when bicycling. There must be awareness supplementing automaticity. By awareness we mean two things: monitoring and steering. In the bicycling example, monitoring means that the rider must pay attention to what is happening in traffic, to the direction in which the road is heading, to any alien objects on the ground, to adjusting his or her velocity to the sharpness of curves, etc. In a sense, all cyclists with normal senses will record everything on their way, but they will not notice everything. The difference between seeing/hearing/sensing on the one hand and noticing on the other is an important element of awareness, involving a change in focus between the whole and the part – or between the forest and the trees. The second thing we mean by awareness, besides this kind of monitoring and observation, is the conscious 'turning-off of the autopilot' to take over control in case of problems, errors or uncertainty. To bring us back to reading, it can be noted, as previously mentioned, that eye movements or saccades are largely automatised during reading. However, fixations are sometimes longer because of a need to 'draw the threads together', and sometimes a reader will make regressions backwards in the text to 'resume the thread'. Such reading behaviour represents manifestations of the steering aspect of awareness.

When a person is reading a simple text on a familiar and interesting subject, automaticity may predominate, but awareness must always be at the ready, monitoring and intervening as and when necessary in the case of problems, errors or uncertainty. It should be noted, though, that it is important to teach young beginning readers to 'take the plunge' without an excessive fear of making mistakes. Kenneth S. Goodman (1994) makes an important point when asserting that '[r]isk-taking has been recognized as a significant aspect of both language learning and proficient language use. In risk-taking there is a necessary balance between tentativeness and self-confidence' (p. 120). On the other hand, children must not learn to rely excessively on the autopilot, either. There must be a proper balance between self-confidence and self-criticism. Reading will be the least effortful and the most rewarding with an optimal combination of automaticity and awareness, because this yields a reading fluency that promotes both an appropriate reading pace and good reading comprehension. There is no mathematical formula for this – rather, it is an attitude acquired through extensive practical training, good role models and a supportive environment.

To this should be added that risk-taking leading to error may yield positive learning. According to the philosopher of science Karl Popper, trial and error is the best route to comprehension and learning in research (Popper, 1959). This can be claimed to apply to all learning. In an educational context, however, it is important to ensure that children will not see their errors or mistakes as failures. Teachers and other adults must draw on their wisdom when making corrections – unless the children detect and correct their own mistakes, which awareness actually often helps them do.

It is also important to ensure that automatisation does not cover only the technical aspects of reading – interpretation and problem-solving also need to be automatised to some extent. Correspondingly, awareness may be needed at all stages of the reading process. As mentioned above, sensing and perception typically happen so quickly that they may be believed to be entirely automatised 'chain reactions', but they also involve the solution of tasks or problems. Indeed, according to Rumelhart as quoted above, there appears to be a continuity between what has been called sensation and perception and what has been called comprehension – sensations are not just patterns of irritations on our sensory surfaces. To delve deeper into this issue, we believe that it is fruitful to make use of hermeneutics, something that in our view has so far not been done to a sufficient extent in reading research. This is probably because reading research has mainly taken place in the English-speaking world while hermeneutics belongs to a Continental European tradition.

Hermeneutics was originally a method for interpreting literary, theological and legal texts. However, it has progressively evolved into a general method of interpretation which can be used, for example, to interpret existence as a whole – that is, as a philosophical method (Gadamer, 1960). On the other hand, it can also be used to interpret the simplest of sensory impressions. The principle remains the same: seeing the whole and the parts in relation to each other. When faced with entirely new and unfamiliar phenomena, people like to begin by trying to achieve a rough overall understanding. This is then used to identify what seem to be relevant details and attempt to understand them. Other details will also be noticed and understood in different ways. As a rule, this understanding of details will affect, and thus change, the understanding of the whole. And this new understanding of the whole may in turn contribute to a new understanding of the parts. This interaction between the whole and the parts is referred to as the hermeneutic circle or spiral. In theory, there can be no such thing as a final, entirely certain and entirely clear understanding of anything: hermeneutics amounts to the constant testing of hypotheses without ever arriving at final answers. In practice, for instance when it comes to the interpretation of sensory impressions, this testing of hypotheses usually stops rather soon; but finding, say, the deepest meaning of an important text often involves quite a few rounds of the hermeneutic circle or spiral. In reading research, there is a great deal of talk about 'comprehension'. Since it is never possible to determine whether this result has been attained, however, it would be better to talk about 'interpretation' instead, given that this represents an open process.

Most investigations of reading comprehension, including the large international ones such as PIRLS and PISA, are based on concrete questions and answers – either open questions and answers, which are assessed and scored by researchers, or multiple-choice questions where students select options. The answers sought sometimes consist in pure facts while other questions require more or less logical or psychological inferences to be made. The tests do not primarily concern the process leading up to the answer, but the answer itself. What is more, 'rational' lines of reasoning characterised by common sense are highly valued while the tests are less well suited to more extreme individuals who either go strictly by logic or have a vivid imagination. This way of measuring (reading) comprehension has characterised psychological and pedagogical research in English-speaking countries.

On the European Continent, by contrast, hermeneutics has been more important (although not yet in the field of reading tests). There, the process – interpretation – is what matters the most. In addition, hermeneutics takes a broader perspective than traditional theories of comprehension in that it covers the entire spectrum from the interpretation of sensory impressions to the interpretation of life experiences. In other words, it is relevant to everything from the psychology of perception to philosophy – including textual analysis. It is true that this process of interpretation is more difficult to measure than the product of comprehension, but even so we are of the opinion that it is more important to focus on that process than on the product traditionally referred to as reading comprehension. This is because hermeneutics can give us a platform or common denominator for the entire reading process, from sensory perception to the interpretation of all the nuances of meaning of individual words and the interpretation of long texts or complex situations as wholes. Someone meeting a person for the first time will interpret that situation and that person using the same method as when interpreting the tiniest sensory impressions for the first time.

As we have seen above, many people – especially of a cognitivist persuasion – claim that reading requires phonological awareness. This is correct in the sense that a reader must know that there is a connection between the phonemes of spoken language and the graphemes of written language. In a sense, we hear all of the sounds in a stream of speech, but we do not notice them all. In initial reading instruction, it is important for children to notice the elements making up the stream of speech. And attention or awareness in the sense of noticing things is also important when sounds are put together to form wholes. If a reader sounds out, say, /s/-/ʌ/-/n/ too slowly, he or she may not notice the similarity between that sound package and the word 'sun' of spoken language. This is a field where children can often be seen to experience Aha! moments – a phenomenon which is in fact closely related to what connectionists call 'emergence'.

Correspondingly, it is important that a reader should not only see the text, but also be able to notice the letters. When someone is noticing details in this manner, awareness predominates over automaticity – and as mentioned, the balance between them must be adapted to the circumstances. A good reader will be able to rely on automaticity to a large extent, but even good readers must make use of awareness when proof-reading.

We mentioned before that the history of reading research started with a visual approach. While that approach has not been particularly prominent after the 1960s, there have been interesting developments in the visual study of reading as well. Above all, it has been found that when readers are fixating, they use the parvocellular system to delve deeper into details. The magnocellular system, by contrast, provides a rougher overall impression, giving information about the required duration of fixations and the appropriate length of saccades between fixations. This can be seen as an ingenious alternation between automaticity and awareness and between a rough impression of wholes and more detailed study of parts.

According to the dual-route model – which has been particularly emphasised by cognitivist reading researchers even though it has been more or less implicitly assumed to exist ever since the beginnings of reading research – there is a direct route from whole words to their meaning and pronunciation, with word recognition taking place automatically. The other route is the one that must be taken when word recognition is not automatic. This dichotomy also corresponds to that between automaticity and awareness. It is important to combine these two routes in an optimal way.

One advantage of bringing hermeneutics – the theory of interpretation – into reading research is, as already mentioned, that it can be used across the range, from the interpretation of sensory impressions and graphemes to the interpretation of entire texts or meanings. An additional advantage is that this extends the focus to encompass the processes involved rather than just the final products or outputs. This makes it possible to find out whether a reader is on the right path – to the extent that there is indeed a right path and a set goal. The disadvantage is that this makes measuring more difficult, but the most important things are in fact often the hardest to measure.

READING FLUENCY

INTRODUCTION

According to Wolf and Katzir-Cohen (2001), the amount of interest paid to reading fluency has varied over the history of reading-instruction theory, with high points during periods when reading aloud has been seen as crucial. Allington (1983) in particular has contributed strongly to the inclusion of fluency as an explicit objective in various national curricula. Such official recognition has given reading aloud a higher status and greater importance in reading instruction. The US National Reading Panel (2000) further reinforced this tendency (cf. Pikulski & Chard, 2005). As we see it, however, there remain two large and challenging questions: what is reading fluency, and how is it best measured? This chapter aims to take a closer look at those two questions. It must be seen in the context of the chapters on reading skill and reading instruction in this book, given the importance of understanding the inter-relationships among reading fluency, reading skill, reading pace and reading comprehension. A key point in this respect is the insight that hermeneutics can bring together sensory impressions from letters and the understanding of meaning.

DIFFERENT VIEWS ON READING FLUENCY

At an early stage of the history of reading-instruction theory, a great deal of emphasis was placed on automatising the technical elements of reading as far as possible (cf., e.g., Huey 1908) so as to achieve good reading fluency. This term (and others) have been used in various, often unclear meanings. According to the National Reading Panel (2000), it is 'a critical component of skilled reading' (p. 32) and 'an essential part of reading' (p. 328) – even though it is not clearly defined. It is also unclear whether this means that fluency should be included in the definition of reading. For example, fluency has so far not been an element of the different variants of – and proposed extensions to – the 'reading formula' (reading = decoding × comprehension) (Gough & Tunmer, 1986).

In practice, good public readers such as actors and news presenters are probably often used as benchmarks to determine what 'reading fluency' means, with flawless and fast reading (aloud) as the common characteristics. Against that background, one might wonder whether aesthetic concerns are also part of the reason why reading fluency is emphasised at school. Further, it is nowadays often stressed that reading aloud should resemble natural speech as far as possible, or rather that reading aloud should be such that it captures and maintains the listener's attention and interest. However, many object to ascribing such importance to the receiver. For example, Harris and Hodges (1985) assert that reading fluency is the 'freedom from word identification problems that might hinder comprehension' (p. 85).

According to another view, reading fluency is seen as the 'bridge' between decoding and comprehension (Chard, Pikulski, & McDonagh, 2006). A person reading unevenly and slowly will have problems with comprehension and thus find it difficult to identify the speech equivalents of written words and sentences. A similar view on reading fluency underlies the CORI educational software (Guthrie, Wigfield, & Perencevich, 2004); it is reflected in the fact that special emphasis is placed on increasing the reading fluency of struggling learners up to a level where their reading pace no longer prevents them from gaining access to content. It is interesting to note that once students have attained that level, reading pace is no longer assigned special importance. Up to a certain level, then, reading fluency will thus presumably promote the reader's own comprehension – as well as that of any listeners. As we will show later, however, the opposite also applies in that reading fluency presupposes a certain level of comprehension.

The direction of any causal relationship between reading comprehension and reading fluency is indeed a moot point. LaBerge and Samuels (1974) go beyond asserting that reading fluency is a mere bridge between decoding and comprehension by specially emphasising that automatisation of the technical elements of reading lead to more attention and energy being devoted to reading comprehension. In line with this, Rasinski and Hoffman (2003) claim that automatisation and correct pronunciation and comprehension are important components of reading comprehension, but add prosody to the list. In reading aloud, like in spoken language, the meaning of a sentence is not just the sum of the meanings of the component words, because the effect of prosody (intonation, stress and rhythm) must be added to this.

Prosody constitutes a condition of meaning specific to spoken language. Its absence from written language means that written text must carry a heavier semantic burden than speech (with some of that burden being allocated to punctuation, which is absent from spoken language). Thus prosody is not only of aesthetic importance, but provides information about the emphasis placed on individual units of meaning and about their grouping together. It is a well-known fact that the meaning contained in a sentence can be altered through modifications to stress, voice quality, intonation and rhythm. Text type also matters greatly – the reading of a poem will have a different prosody from the reading of a political manifesto – and so do the situation and purpose of reading. According to Miller and Schwanenflugel (2006), prosody contributes positively to reading comprehension beyond its importance for correct and quick word recognition. While prosody as such is not a norm, but rather a tool to describe characteristics of spoken language in terms of stress, intonation and rhythm, prosodic characteristics can in practice come to be associated with various expressive ideals of a more or less normative character, such as that of reading aloud in a 'natural-sounding' way. Here, too, however, the direction of the causal relationship becomes unclear. Consequently, even though prosody is a relatively well-defined concept of phonology, it does not help much when it comes to clarifying the meaning of reading fluency. Indeed, prosody may well be definable, but it is hard to say what prosodic characteristics are correct in a given situation or in the reading of specific types of text. The measurement of prosody and thus of reading fluency will therefore be subjective and qualitative. To this should be added the question of whether prosody is not rather a manifestation of comprehension – is it not the case that only when someone has understood the content of a written utterance will he or she be able to add appropriate prosody to the various parts of that utterance?

Rasinski (1990) claims that the typical approach to instruction in prosody and reading fluency has been for the teacher to read first in an exemplary manner and for students to imitate. Technical aids have also been made use of in this context (cf. Johnston, 2006). Once the teacher has read a text, the student will read the same text and be corrected until the result is satisfactory. However, such imitation may easily become both artificial, mechanical and automatised in a way that will make the student shift the emphasis to the exterior and the surface, which may hinder rather than facilitate comprehension. Hoffman (1987) therefore warned against this type of imitation and reading aloud; and according to Altweger, Jordan and Shelton (2007), this is why reading fluency is not, and should not be, given much room in modern reading instruction. What is more, the transferability of the results of the method for training prosody is an open question: to what extent will they apply only to the text trained? Should not reading fluency be something that is adapted to the circumstances obtaining in the individual case? Perhaps it is better to measure this mainly in relation to new, unfamiliar texts?

Based on what has been said about prosody, it can be claimed that to the extent that reading fluency can be measured, such measurement must above all be based on reading aloud. But does that mean that reading fluency can be defined only in relation to reading aloud? If reading fluency promotes reading comprehension, it should presumably be aimed for in silent reading as well. Surely, the claim made by the National Reading Panel (2000) that reading fluency is an essential part of reading (p. 328) must apply to silent reading, too? We have discussed the role of prosody in the evaluation of reading fluency, but it seems that prosody is irrelevant for silent reading. Then the issue of reading fluency is reduced to a question of reading pace, or possibly of reading pace in relation to scores on reading-comprehension measurements taken immediately after reading. If the concept of reading fluency is to cover all reading (both silent reading and reading aloud), the situation described above makes it difficult to define and measure. Further, an exclusive focus on pace is not appropriate, either, because it is not possible to read faster than one thinks. Against the backdrop of these circumstances, we find it appropriate to suggest that (good) reading fluency might mean *thinking one's way through a text without the written medium obstructing one's thought*. Such an idea is close to the view of Harris and Hodges (1985). In that case, reading fluency will have to be defined individually and situationally – in the light of the person and circumstances concerned – and not in relation to group or national standards.

As mentioned, reading instruction has traditionally placed a great deal of emphasis on reading aloud. Obviously one important reason for this is that it allows students' decoding skills to be tested. However, less importance has been attached to testing comprehension, and it was often forgotten that students devoted so much attention to reading aloud in a correct or elegant manner that they had correspondingly less focus on comprehension (Hyatt, 1943). Yet Huey (1908) argued early on that more weight had to be assigned to students' individual silent reading, which can both be faster and yield better comprehension than reading aloud, and which also facilitates individual adjustment and enhances motivation. Based on these ideas, some authors advised against internal 'pronunciation' during silent reading (McDade, 1937; Rohrer, 1943). It can be questioned whether this represents an appropriate understanding of silent reading, but we will not delve deeper into this issue here. However, it is interesting to note that less weight being placed on reading aloud traditionally results in less weight being placed on reading fluency as well. According to Rasinski and Hoffman (2003), reading aloud is the best way to promote reading fluency. On the other hand, Allington (1983) claims that silent reading is the best way to promote comprehension. These two countervailing claims make it obvious that there is a need for a clearer concept of reading fluency during silent reading.

As mentioned above, reading fluency is also understood, to some extent, as a matter of reading pace. This underpins several of the positions referred to above: any position emphasising automatisation will also emphasise pace. What several of those positions may seem to be lacking, however, is the insight that the pace must be adapted to the circumstances. In this chapter, we will maintain our hypothesis of reading fluency as thinking one's way through a text without being obstructed by the written medium precisely because it allows for the adjustment of pace to circumstances. This hypothesis thus also tempers the widespread idea equating reading fluency with a quick reading pace, opening for new ways to think about reading fluency. The need for more nuanced thinking about reading fluency is particularly urgent given the software on offer to schools from commercial players which generally go very far in equating reading pace and reading fluency. However, we will not devote any attention to such applications in the present chapter except by evoking the need for ideas about fluency that differ from those represented by such software.

HOW DOES READING FLUENCY MANIFEST ITSELF?

In 1974, LaBerge and Samuels stressed the importance of reading fluency, but with the primary aim of automatising visual perception, the identification of letters and sounds, the bringing together of sounds, etc. (LaBerge & Samuels, 1974). Their idea was that inadequate automatisation of these tasks draws attention and energy away from comprehension efforts. Stanovich (1980) and Perfetti (1985) express similar ideas, with automatisation and energy efficiency as keywords. While they draw upon behaviourist thinking, their objective is to promote the cognitive processes, particularly comprehension. This means that reading fluency is intended to promote cognitive aspects. However, it is rarely mentioned that cognitive aspects can promote reading fluency, too.

Stanovich makes a distinction between bottom-up and top-down processes. The former start with the perception of letters and end with the comprehension of words or larger units of text. This 'route' is associated with the Phonics school of reading-instruction theory. The latter processes go the opposite way and are more closely linked to the Whole Language school (cf. our chapters on reading skill and reading instruction in this book), according to which readers make assumptions about the meaning of words based on their context and the purpose of the text, such that it may not be necessary to decode or read each word in detail. Stanovich (1980) is of the opinion that starting from context must entail slow and highly effortful reading. Those who choose this strategy because they have difficulties placing building-blocks on top of each other using the bottom-up approach will, in all likelihood, read with greater uncertainty and make more mistakes than those who have a certain and automatised mastery of the bottom-up approach. In our view, however, it cannot be excluded that those who have automatised those basic skills will start 'at the top' with meaning and context; we see this as a good illustration of the artificial opposition between Phonics and Whole Language. Pressley (2006) has tried to find an intermediate position between these two opposite schools, an attempt that we will comment on in greater detail later (see also Chapter 7).

Automatic, fast and correct identification of the pronunciation and meaning of individual words can be seen, at most, as a necessary condition for reading fluency, but not as a sufficient condition because reading fluency applies to entire sentences and even larger chunks of text. What is more, automatic and fast identification of individual words may easily lead to mechanical reading and does not ensure that reading produces coherent wholes. For readers to attain correct prosody, for example, there is a need for a comprehension of the whole to determine, to some extent, how smaller parts should be read. The top-down approach must thus be applied to some degree. However, as is clear from our chapters on reading skill and reading instruction in this book, all reading – and hence all reading fluency – must be based on the alternation between focusing on the whole and focusing on the parts.

LaBerge and Samuels (1974) and Stanovich (1980) have made important contributions to the debate on reading fluency. However, we have two important objections or additions: (1) their view of automatisation is problematic in that they do not see automaticity and awareness in context (see, e.g., Tønnessen, 1999, 2011); and (2) interpretation and comprehension should be based to a larger extent on the hermeneutic tradition, which has so far played a more important role on the European Continent than in the pedagogy, psychology and philosophy of English-speaking countries.

It is true that LaBerge and Samuels (1974) probably make an important point in their claim that humans can direct their attention to only one thing at a time and that the automatisation of the 'technical' tasks of reading makes it possible to devote a maximum of attention to comprehension. However, it must be kept in mind that complete automatisation is neither possible nor desirable. The idea of reading fluency as being able to think one's way through a text without being obstructed by the written medium, elaborated upon earlier in this chapter, internalises that insight from LaBerge and Samuels (1974), but without making it into an either/or choice between automaticity and awareness. All skills are performed through a situationally determined alternation between automaticity and awareness, the latter meaning that people monitor their performance and intervene as needed in the case of errors or problems. New and difficult tasks require more awareness than familiar tasks. Possessing a skill to a high level means being able to achieve an optimal alternation between automaticity and awareness, taking account of the requirements of the situation. One example is riding a bicycle. This is an activity that people tend to automatise to a large extent, but riding at high velocity on an unfamiliar and rugged path requires a high level of awareness. Someone who trusts the 'autopilot' too much in such a situation will easily end up with problems that are difficult to solve. Further, a gymnast drawing excessively on automaticity may produce an overly mechanical performance – even though it may be technically flawless (an aesthetic aspect which, as mentioned before, can be argued to apply to reading fluency as well).

FROM BALANCED APPROACH TO HERMENEUTICS

As mentioned, the main emphasis of Phonics is on the bottom-up approach while that of Whole Language is on the top-down approach. In our view, those two approaches must be combined. A person who has successfully automatised the bottom-up processes (of decoding) is in a good position to become a fluent reader, but to the extent that fluency includes mastery of prosody, that person must also understand units larger than words. For example, correct use in reading aloud of the falling intonation signalling the end of a declarative sentence which is found in many languages, including Norwegian and English, presupposes an understanding of the sentence as a whole. A sentence whose function is to ask a question will not have that intonation but will instead be given another characteristic intonation with a rise on the last word. Further, questions often have a syntactic structure which indicates early on in the sentence that they are indeed questions, for example an interrogative pronoun or (in the case of Norwegian and some other Germanic languages) the main verb at the very beginning of the sentence. Recognition of such markers, and the implementation of the associated prosodic features, requires both long experience and a highly active form of reading. To read aloud in a manner resembling natural speech, a person must read actively, alternately focusing on the part and the whole – that is, focusing both on the pronunciation of each word and on its context. On this view of fluency, the most frequent cases of fluency breakdown during reading aloud will be those where the reader is preoccupied with the word just being read but fails to take in the function of the utterance. In such cases, readers are likely to realise their mistake immediately and will often produce a new version with correct prosody afterwards. Hence the top-down approach comes into play here in a certain sense and to a certain degree; we are of the opinion that general hermeneutic principles apply, meaning that the whole is understood in the light of the parts, and vice versa.

Those principles can be illustrated by a person trying to understand a poem, who has to start with a rough understanding of the whole to make sense as far as possible of the individual words. This can be said to constitute an assumption or a hypothesis. Once the meanings of the individual words have been identified, it is likely that the understanding of the whole will change as a result. Such change to the hypothesis or overall understanding corresponds to the way in which a scientific hypothesis may be modified after encountering reality. Logically speaking, the structure or approach is the same: a new understanding of the whole forms the basis for new readings and new ways of understanding the details, which, in turn, will change the understanding of the whole again. This process is referred to as the hermeneutic circle or spiral. It is used not only to interpret texts – the same method is actually used to interpret sensory impressions. Faced with the task of interpreting unclear handwriting, for example, it is a good idea to start from an understanding of the whole. In this sense, good reading will constantly combine bottom-up and top-down processes. This can be seen as a combination of the schools of Phonics and Whole Language from the field of reading-instruction theory, but the way they are combined differs from the way suggested in the 'balanced view' recommended by Pressley (2006).

Automatised use of the bottom-up approach may quickly come across as mechanical; an extreme example is hyperlexia, which involves very fast decoding with few mistakes but minimal comprehension. In our opinion, the reflections presented above provide additional support for the view of reading fluency as the bridge between decoding and comprehension. At the same time, however, it should be noted that a certain amount of reading fluency will promote comprehension; a person reading slowly and unevenly will have difficulties with interconnections and comprehension, never really 'getting into the text'. Samuels and Farstrup (2006) are right to claim that comprehension and reading fluency have a mutual impact on each other and that it is hard to say which of them comes first. Further, it is clear that the purpose and nature of a text as well as motivational factors influence reading fluency. Exposure to a wide range of different reading situations and texts is important for the development of maximum flexibility and reading fluency.

FOCUSING ON READING FLUENCY IN EDUCATION

The lines of reasoning followed in this chapter have certain ramifications for the possible role of reading fluency in education. One main implication is that there should be a strong focus on increasing the reading pace and automatising word recognition until a reading level is reached where the written medium no longer obstructs the students from thinking their way forward in the text. This is what we see as reading fluency. On this view, reading fluency includes reading pace, but it does not exclusively concern reading pace. Once the threshold has been passed, the individual has entered a 'fluency zone' with a potential for further development. That zone will vary depending on the challenges faced.

A second important implication of our reasoning is that, as students advance to higher years and levels, progressively less emphasis should be placed on reading pace. This is because an important task of education is to teach students to notice things in texts and to relate to texts and text elements of varying degrees of difficulty with a view to comprehension. Indeed, it may well be a greater challenge to make, say, upper-secondary students read slowly enough, with attention, than to make them read faster. We have also pointed to the aesthetic dimension, where reading fluency in aesthetic and prosodic terms will overlap with learning goals in the fields of presentation techniques and argumentation. That aspect of reading fluency will be a natural element of education, particularly in higher years. Against this backdrop, there is limited value to having upper-secondary – or other relatively senior – students undergo tests that primarily measure reading pace. Such tests may actually give teachers, students and parents the wrong signals about the reading challenges that students encounter in the years concerned, and also about what reading really is. To this should be added the existence of commercial players offering products, often at a steep price, said to increase students' reading pace. Many such products have a documented effect on reading pace, and for some of them there is also evidence of simple relationships between use of the product and reading comprehension.

When it comes to the present offer on the Norwegian market, there are fundamental objections to be made against this type of documentation. The problem is not primarily that the effects are small or non-existent, but rather the very absence of critical reflection on how teachers, students and parents should use the information and on how it might be part of knowledge about what reading is. Speed-reading courses probably do make their participants read faster (even though some studies show little or no effect), but the main content of such courses consists of general learning and reading strategies that good teachers also use on an everyday basis, although perhaps not always to their full potential. And speed-reading courses are probably also able to accelerate the reading pace of people who have no real reason to be slow readers. This can be explained by reference to the fact that each person has a range for the performance of reading skill within which performance can be more or less optimal. Further, in a best-case scenario, some participants in such courses will also make discoveries leading them to develop more strategic reading. However, this is exactly what good teachers do every day at school, and – unlike the commercial players – teachers also present this as part of an overall understanding of the development of reading. Moreover, schools are offered software based exclusively on strict behaviourist ideas, but without the behaviourist reflections on what reading is. If such software is used on an everyday basis at schools without a very good awareness of how it might promote reading skill, there is cause for concern.

A recent study shows that adult dyslectics read faster and with better comprehension when they are pushed to speed up their reading (Breznitz et al., 2013). That study used computer software showing sentences on the screen with the letters moving to from left to right at a set pace and disappearing off the screen, forcing the reader to speed up. After completing a task, the reader was asked a comprehension question. If he or she gave a correct answer, each letter in the next sentence would be shown on the screen for 2 milliseconds less. If the answer was wrong, the exposure time did not change. There is of course a limit to how fast anyone can read, which is why the training was organised in sessions. What is interesting about this approach is the mechanism (the comprehension question) linking the reading pace to the level of comprehension at a fundamental level. In addition, this study gives a perspective on our point that the performance of reading skill takes place within a range and that the development of reading skill involves expanding and moving the upper limits of that range (see also our chapter on reading skill in this book). This means that the method used in the above-mentioned study can be seen as a method for adjusting the reading pace to the circumstances, the objective being the further development of reading skill.

In this chapter, we have proposed a hypothesis about reading fluency understood as thinking oneself through a text without being obstructed by the written medium. This requires an interplay between the whole and the parts and is thus linked at a fundamental level to the individual performance of reading skill, which is a prerequisite for the development of reading skill itself.

There is widespread agreement among researchers and practitioners alike that reading fluency is important, but definitions are both unclear and varying. There is no doubt that uneven and slow reading makes it difficult to take an overview and thus to find out what a text corresponds to in natural speech. Reading fluency thus promotes reading comprehension, but – as we have seen – reading comprehension also promotes reading fluency. Isolated reading aloud, with an exclusive emphasis on pronunciation and prosody, may become superficial and mechanical. Such exercises may also draw attention away from reading comprehension. Further, reading fluency includes an aesthetic component, but this must not be cultivated for the sake of its aesthetic value. A speed-skater chooses flexibility and style because this increases velocity: aesthetics and effectiveness form a unit. This should also be the case for reading fluency and reading comprehension.

READING INSTRUCTION

INTRODUCTION

The debate on the methods of initial reading instruction has probably been the most intense in the United States, where the positions may also have been the most entrenched. In our own country, Norway, and generally in Scandinavia, the camps have been less rigidly opposed to each other. To this should be added that the Norwegian spelling conventions, dialect situation and cultural and educational circumstances have affected the characteristics of the national debate. However, given that the underlying pedagogical principles are similar, we will here account for some of the main developments of the debate in the United States.

Most commentators tend to refer to two main positions, using somewhat different names for them. Here we will call one of those camps Phonics and the other Whole Language. However, it should be kept in mind what Chall (1967) found after reviewing 85 studies of teaching methods, namely that '[i]t was what the teacher did with the method, the materials, and the children rather than the method itself that seemed to make the difference' (p. 270). This is important not only because any method will be interpreted and practised differently by different teachers, but also because the teacher's personality and the classroom environment may be crucial to the students' learning outcomes.

In Norway, Reading Based on Speech (or LTG) was a popular method in the field of initial reading instruction from the 1970s to the 1990s. This method has some affinities with the Phonics–Whole Language debate but also exhibits certain characteristics and underlying explanations that fall outside that debate. In this chapter, we will focus mainly on Phonics versus Whole Language, because in our opinion this best illustrates the fundamental positions and points of disagreement. However, we will begin with some brief information about LTG and a few comments on it.

The LTG method was developed in the 1970s by the Swedish primary-school teacher Ulrika Leimar (Leimar, 1974). Her starting point was that initial reading instruction at the time was characterised by an artificial and restricted vocabulary (corresponding rather well to the criticism levelled by the Whole Language school at the Phonics school in the United States). She wanted to bring the vocabulary used closer to what the children already knew when first starting school – not primarily include more literary texts. The aim was to integrate meaning and motivation in the learning of the technical skills required for reading. This was a reaction on her part to a predominant Phonics-type tradition, and she was seen as an opponent of that tradition. However, the main reason for her reaction was in fact the way in which that tradition was being practised, and today many would probably place her in between the two US traditions. As evidence, consider the following quotation (Leimar, 1974):

> That first autumn when I was trying out the method (1969/1970), I was not sufficiently aware to what extent it is necessary to draw the children's attention to character–sound correspondences. As a result, in their uninhibited activity in October, the children started guessing words wildly in spontaneous whole-word reading. To remedy such look-and-guess tendencies, I started letting the children analyse the words and experiment with them […] It seems to me that exclusive whole-word reading may not be recommendable at the initial stage. The children must be taught to sound written words together based on an analysis of the sounds in their own, spoken words […] They must be taught a technique to approach even texts that are unfamiliar to them. (p. 40; our translation)

Below we will briefly present (1) the Whole Language tradition and (2) the Phonics tradition, and then (3) examine whether, and if so how, confrontation between these two traditions can be avoided.

THE WHOLE LANGUAGE TRADITION

It is a moot point when Whole Language – in some version or other – was brought into reading instruction in the United States, but at the end of the 19th century there was a reaction to a long-standing tradition in initial instruction where the focus was on short and typically meaningless syllables such as 'ba', 'bi', 'bo', 'bu'. Both teachers and parents felt it was too long before the children engaged in any meaningful reading, fearing that this might undermine their interest and motivation. Reading instruction at the time involved a great deal of drilling and superficial testing. The main method for assessing the children's skills was reading aloud. The linguistic and literary quality of the texts used was low, both because the teachers did not want to depart too far from the children's everyday language and because there was a limited supply of study materials. Moreover, no particular attention was paid to the depth or quality of the children's comprehension. Reading was seen as a technical skill and a practical tool – not as a gateway to the world of language and culture.

As an alternative to that method, an increasing number of people were of the opinion that children should start by learning the connection between entire 'images' of written words – primarily short and highly frequent ones – and their meanings. Subsequently, the idea was for the children progressively to learn how to analyse these written images into letters (graphemes) to be associated with language sounds (phonemes). However, the progression of such instruction could well be somewhat random and often lacked a strong basis in research. Then, from the 1920s onwards, the learning principles of behaviourism became predominant (Rodgers, 2001). Behaviourists wanted to explain all human behaviour in terms of external, observable events, meaning that phenomena such as awareness and thoughts were excluded from study. Reading was explained, in particular, with reference to automatisation.

The 'Sputnik Shock' of 1957 resulted in increased spending on both education and research in the United States, and this also had an impact on reading research and reading instruction. Teachers, parents and researchers debated with increasing intensity which method of initial reading instruction was the most effective and efficient. More careful reflection was carried out to underpin and refine the Whole Language tradition referred to above, according to which learning to link entire written-word images with their associated meanings is more important than starting from the component parts of the words and understanding their structure. Advocates of Whole Language claim that children must also learn to place the words in broader linguistic contexts to be able to find the correct meaning. Kenneth S. Goodman and Frank Smith became the most influential representatives of this movement, and also those who went farthest in their thinking.

According to Yetta M. Goodman and Kenneth S. Goodman (1994), '[r]eading is not simply knowing sounds, words, sentences, and the abstract parts of language that can be studied by linguists. Reading, like listening, consists of processing language and constructing meaning. The reader brings a great deal of information to this complex and active process' (p. 112).

Goodman and Goodman further claim that '[a]s readers make use of their knowledge of all the language cues, they predict, make inferences, select significant features, confirm, and constantly work toward constructing a meaningful text. Not only are they constructing meaning. They are constructing themselves as readers' (p. 115). This view – from a cognitivist perspective focusing on meaning and thus on the similarities between spoken and written language – underscores the importance of understanding and constructing meaningful units and wholes. By contrast, other cognitivists, such as Shankweiler and Liberman (1989), focus on decoding (that is, the technical sides of reading) and consequently stress the differences between listening and reading.

Goodman and Goodman (1994) consider that breaking down spoken language not only risks making the details overshadow the whole, but that the demands placed on the children's ability for abstract thinking are also great – it is always easier to understand a detail if it is placed in a context or shown as part of a whole:

> Through miscue analysis we have learned that, other things being equal, short language sequences are harder to comprehend than are long ones. Sentences are easier than words, paragraphs easier than sentences, pages easier than paragraphs, and stories easier than pages. (p. 121)

Meaning is not something clear and final that a text gives its readers – they have to use their creativity and their power of empathy to find the most meaningful wholes in which the parts can be included:

> The power of language users to fill knowledge gaps with missing elements, to infer unstated meanings and underlying structures, and to deal with novel experiences, novel thoughts, and novel emotions derives from the ability to

predict, to guess, to make choices, to take risks, to go beyond observable data. We must have the capability of being wrong lest the limits on our functioning be too narrowly constrained. Unlike the computer, people do not exhibit specifically programmed, totally dependable responses time after time. We are tentative, we act impulsively, we make mistakes, and we tolerate our own deviations and the mistakes of others. (p. 104)

And nor do readers arrive at meaning by following rules. They have to try different ways, and they must dare to make mistakes:

Everything people do, they do imperfectly. This is not a flaw but an asset. If we always performed perfectly, we could not maintain the tentativeness and flexibility that characterize human learning and the ways we interact with our environment and with one another. This model of imperfection causes us as researchers not to worry about why people fall short of perfection; rather, we are concerned with why people do what they do and with what we can learn about language processes from observing such phenomena [...]. (p. 104)

The way readers arrive at meaning and at wholes is by formulating and testing hypotheses – which is also, incidentally, the way science progresses. Goodman (1967) has referred to this approach, somewhat drastically, as a 'guessing game'. Even though Goodman emphasises that attaining meaning is the primary aim of reading, he does not deny that it may be necessary to break words down into graphemes and phonemes. A reader faced with an unfamiliar word cannot always just guess – he or she must sometimes search for an answer.

Smith (1971) largely shares Goodman's view of reading and of the learning and teaching of it. In his opinion, phonemes and graphemes – the smallest building-blocks – are too abstract for many children, who must learn to see them in broader contexts. At a general level, he asserts that '[t]he psycholinguistic perspective had a number of influences on the field of reading. First, it encouraged us to value literacy experiences that focused on making meaning. This meant that many classroom activities – particularly work-sheets and games which focused on enabling skills such as specific letter-sound correspondences, syllabification activities, structural analysis skills, specific comprehension activities, or study skills – were devalued' (p. 29). Further, the focus on the students' activities entailed a corresponding toning-down of the teacher's importance: the teacher's role was presented not so much as teaching the students to read but as helping them read. The children must indeed learn to read by reading – but the teachers must be ready both to motivate and to correct. Further, reading must not be reduced to a technique. Linguistic awareness and literary taste are overall objectives of a reading instruction that takes as its starting point not only whole *words* but also whole *language*.

THE PHONICS TRADITION

Whole Language was seen as a liberation from superficial, drill-based reading instruction. And there is of course no doubt that teaching children the meanings of whole-word images can be helpful to them on their way to becoming good readers. However, there are some objections to it. First, this approach can also degenerate into drill; and second, it does not make children wholly self-reliant readers because they still have to learn how to analyse word images and what the basic principles of written language are. While these aspects are not entirely neglected by the Whole Language tradition, many think it does not pay enough attention to them.

The alternative is the Phonics tradition. But what characterises that tradition? Adams (1990) finds that question difficult to answer:

> What if we restrict attention to the programs that are centered on phonics? Can we extract an operational definition of the endeavor from them? The answer is no or, at least, not easily. The problem is that there exist many, many such programs – each of Robert Aukerman's books cite over 100. To be sure, a central tenet of each of these programs is that working knowledge of the letter-to-sound correspondences underlying our system of writing is key to proficient reading. Beyond that, however, they differ greatly. (p. 51)

Some of the first – and most prominent – representatives of the Phonics movement assert that, in written language, '[m]eanings are not conveyed directly by signals that differ holistically, but rather by words that are distinct from each other in their internal structure. This structure is formed of a small number of meaningless phonological segments we know as consonants and vowels, and governed according to a highly systematic combinatorial scheme called phonology' (Shankweiler & Liberman, 1989, p. 7). The relationship between letters (or graphemes) and language sounds (or phonemes) varies between languages. Some languages, such as Finnish, are entirely regular in that a letter is pronounced in the same way in all contexts. English is one of the least regular languages in this respect (cf. Seymour, 2005). Hence English-speaking children learning how to pronounce letters have to learn a great many exceptions. There is obvious variation in how they learn this – as is clear from the claim that upwards of 75 per cent of children will learn to read regardless of the method being used, often without particularly explicit instruction (Shankweiler & Liberman, 1989). In other words, they discover connections between spoken and written words on their own, through experience with written texts.

Phonics stresses the importance of children attaining phonemic awareness. Children perceive spoken words as wholes but have to learn that those wholes consist of discrete sounds. This is the only way for them to learn what the individual letters represent. Once they have learned that, they can break down a written image into its component letters and associate sounds with those letters, meaning that they understand that the word 'sun' consists of three letters corresponding to the three sounds /s/ + /ʌ/ + /n/. Bringing those three sounds together yields a whole corresponding to the word 'sun' of spoken language. But if the children pronounce this too slowly or put the stress in the wrong place, the task of finding out what it corresponds to in spoken language becomes more difficult.

The US National Reading Panel (2000) defines phonemic awareness as the ability to focus on and manipulate phonemes in spoken words. Phonemic awareness can be measured in a series of ways, including by testing the ability to identify the first sound in a word, sounds common to several words or words distinguishing themselves from each other by their first sound, combining isolated sounds into words, breaking up a word into its component sounds, or identifying the word that will remain after a sound has been removed from another word (National Reading Panel, 2000, pp. 2–1 ff.).

While there are many studies indicating that such tests or exercises do measure or promote phonemic awareness, it can be questioned to what extent they do not also measure or require other intellectual skills. It is clear that the tasks involved demand a great deal of concentration, abstraction and motivation. Many children may also have difficulty understanding the purpose of such tasks. Still, despite these reservations, a series of studies indicate that Phonics is an effective and efficient method of initial reading instruction; the National Reading Panel (2000) has compiled one of the most recent and most extensive overviews of its use and effectiveness. However, as mentioned by Adams in the quotation above, there is significant variation in the content and use of this method. For example, there is no consensus when it comes to for how long or to what extent the method should be used, nor as regards how much account should be taken of individual factors. It is also unknown to what extent this method promotes a desire to read or a sense of linguistic and literary quality.

BALANCED INSTRUCTION

According to Gaffney and Anderson (2000), Whole Language was at its most popular in the United States from the mid-1980s to the mid-1990s. Cowen (2003) presents and evaluates six research reports on initial reading instruction published between 1967 and 2000 – Bond and Dykstra (1967), Chall (1967), Anderson, Hiebert, Scott and Wilkinson (1985), Adams (1990), Snow, Burns and Griffin (1998) and National Reading Panel (2000) – concluding that all of them take a 'balanced' view on the relationship between Whole Language and Phonics. This is correct insofar as none of the six reports is extreme or obviously biased, but it must be said that Cowen uses 'balanced' in varying and unclear meanings.

A more recent evaluation, that by Pressley (2006), was based on classroom studies, which sets it apart from many others. Today he may be the person primarily associated with the concept of a 'balanced view' on reading instruction. We will therefore briefly highlight some of his findings and thoughts. First, he notes that '[l]iteracy instruction in the top three classrooms was exceptionally well balanced with respect to the elements of whole language – reading of outstanding literature, writing – and the explicit teaching of skills' (p. 252). Here it would seem that 'balanced' is above all used to refer to the amounts and proportions of the two methods, and this also seems to be the case in the following quotation:

The radical middle proposed here is only radical in contrast to the extreme whole-language and phonics positions that have defined the recent debates about beginning-reading instruction. There are a number of scholars before us (e.g., Adams, 1990; Cazden, 1992; Chall, 1967, 1983; Delpit, 1986; Duffy, 1991; Fisher & Hiebert, 1990; McCaslin, 1989) who have proposed that the most sensible beginning-reading curriculum should be a balance of skills development and authentic reading and writing. The unique contribution of the work of our group is in demonstrating that is really what good teachers do. (p. 280)

Balancing and combining in this sense is of course important, but it is easy to form the impression that the goals set and activities undertaken are entirely different in nature: on the one side (Phonics), technical skills are being promoted; while on the other (Whole Language), the aim is to promote a desire to read as well as linguistic and cultural tastes. This should mean that the proportion of Phonics will be progressively reduced in favour of Whole Language as the children acquire the fundamental skills.

However, the issue of balancing can also be seen from the perspective of how reading is defined. As we understand it, that is the approach underpinning the following claim by Pressley (2006):

Some who have thought about meaning making during reading seem to think that meaning making occurs from the bottom up. For them, reading is about the processing of letters and words. Meaning making is sounding out the words, which are listened to by the mind. Indeed, there is a long history of distinguished research establishing that even when good readers read silently, there is something of a speech process involved [...] Others who think about meaning making during reading think that it occurs from the top down. That is, based on world knowledge, people have hypotheses about what the text is going to say, and this prior knowledge goes far in explaining comprehension (Anderson & Pearson, 1984). (p. 59)

Pressley's view is that there is an intermediate position between the bottom-up and top-down approaches, where both of those approaches are involved in the construction of meaning (or meaning-making) from a text. Here the bottom-up approach is seen as the central feature of Phonics while the top-down one is correspondingly seen as central to Whole Language. In our opinion, however, this is not just an intermediate position but amounts to the integration of the two approaches – depending on how the two approaches are seen.

The bottom-up approach in reading entails taking the written image as the starting point and noticing what elements it consists of. The first step is thus visual sensing, followed by interpretation through visual perception. This interpretation is based on memory as well as on a whole in which the sensory impression is placed – in the case of reading, letters are seen in relation to words and larger units of meaning. It happens so fast that people rarely associate these fundamental

CHAPTER 7

processes with meaning, but the connectionist Rumelhart would appear to do so, considering his use of terminology:

> I use the term perception rather freely here. In general, it is my opinion that the distinction between the perceptual and conceptual aspects of reading is not that useful. As I will suggest later, there appears to be a continuity between what has been called perception and what has been called comprehension. My use of the term perception in the present context is simply the use of the one term to cover the entire process. (Rumelhart, 1994, p. 893)

In our opinion, it might be even more fruitful to use hermeneutics, which is a general theory about interpretation and meaning. It has been particularly prominent on the European Continent – especially in Germany and France. The reason why it has hardly made an appearance in reading research may well be the predominance in that field of researchers from the English-speaking world. The fundamental idea of hermeneutics is that the whole and the part must always be understood in relation to each other. Someone who encounters an unfamiliar phenomenon will typically first try to place it in a broader context. When, say, reading a poem for the first time, a reader will perhaps ask him- or herself whether it is part of a major collection of poems or written by a major poet. The reader may also want general information about the author and the poem – cultural background, year of writing, intended readership, etc. This yields a rough overall understanding, which the reader will use to identify important parts and to attain an initial understanding of them. That understanding, in turn, will be used to adjust and refine the understanding of the whole, which will then be used to achieve a better understanding of the details. This alternation between the whole and the parts is called the hermeneutic circle or spiral; it means that it is never possible to attain a final and completely clear understanding of anything. This method was originally used to interpret theological, legal and literary texts, but it has since come into more general use. In fact, this method is used to try to understand people, actions – indeed the whole of existence. What is more, it is also used to interpret sensory impressions, which is why it is misleading to claim that reading occupies an intermediate position between sensing and comprehension. In line with hermeneutics – and with Rumelhart and others – it is better to talk in terms of an interaction between the whole and the parts.

But what does this mean for classroom practices? The distinction between Whole Language and Phonics roughly corresponds to that between implicit teaching and learning and explicit teaching and learning. Studies of emergent literacy show that children are capable of acquiring both phonemic awareness and a sense of linguistic and literary quality without explicit instruction. Indeed, Shankweiler and Liberman's above-mentioned claim that 75 per cent of children will learn to read regardless of the method used could indicate that the distinction between the two methods is artificial. The solution, in our view, does not involve mixing the two methods in set proportions but rather in dissolving the distinction between them. However, this does not mean that our solution is methodlessness.

90

Rather, creativity must be harnessed to ensure that approaches suitable to individual learners are constantly being developed and tried out.

The biggest problem in present-day reading instruction may be intellectualisation and abstraction, introduced as a result of a rather extreme interpretation of the concepts of phonemic awareness and metacognition (thinking about thinking). Children do need to learn about the relationships between phonemes and graphemes, but as far as possible this must be achieved by means of concrete examples. The old rule according to which people learn to read by reading has a good deal of truth to it, and so does the rule about learning through trial and error. One of the teacher's most important tasks is to correct and motivate in the best possible way. This is more art than technique. The teacher's personality is often more important than the methods used.

CHAPTER 8

CONCLUDING REFLECTIONS

INTRODUCTION

While there is an extensive literature both in the field of philosophy of psychology and in that of philosophy of education, hardly any published philosophical reflection has been devoted to reading and dyslexia research (among the few exceptions, I would like to mention Helland and Rommetveit, 2006, and Elliott and Gibbs, 2008). The amount of empirical research into reading and dyslexia has increased greatly, but there has been little theoretical thinking to accompany that increase. In order to look back upon the research undertaken and evaluate it with a view to the future, it is necessary to introduce additional theoretical considerations of a more profound nature. In this book, I have tried to deal with a number of themes of topical interest. I would like to use these concluding reflections to emphasise and elaborate on some of my main points. It is of course impossible to present all nuances, reservations and grounds, but I do hope that I will be able to describe my ideas clearly enough to stimulate further reflection.

HAS PROGRESS BEEN MADE IN READING AND DYSLEXIA RESEARCH?

State of the art in 2000

In 1997, the United States Congress decided to appoint a committee called the National Reading Panel, which was given the task of investigating the impact of various methods in initial reading instruction. The Panel reported in April 2000. The title of its report was *Teaching Children to Read* and its subtitle was *An Evidence-Based Assessment of the Scientific Research Literature on Reading and Its Implications for Reading Instruction.*
The following quotation is taken from the report summary:

The Panel considered roughly 100,000 reading studies published since 1966, and another 10,000 published before that time. From this pool, the Panel selected several hundred studies for its review and analysis. The National Reading Panel's analysis made it clear that the best approach to reading instruction is one that incorporates:

– Explicit instruction in phonemic awareness
– Systematic phonics instruction
– Methods to improve fluency
– Ways to enhance comprehension

The Panel found that a combination of techniques is effective for teaching children to read:

– *Phonemic awareness* – the knowledge that spoken words can be broken apart into smaller segments of sound known as phonemes. Children who are read to at home – especially material that rhymes – often develop the basis of phonemic awareness. Children who are not read to will probably need to be taught that words can be broken apart into smaller sounds.

– *Phonics* – the knowledge that letters of the alphabet represent phonemes, and that these sounds are blended together to form written words. Readers who are skilled in phonics can sound out words they haven't seen before, without first having to memorize them.

– *Fluency* – the ability to recognize words easily, read with greater speed, accuracy, and expression, and to better understand what is read. Children gain fluency by practicing reading until the process becomes automatic; guided oral repeated reading is one approach to helping children become fluent readers.

– *Guided oral reading* – reading out loud while getting guidance and feedback from skilled readers. The combination of practice and feedback promotes reading fluency.

– *Teaching vocabulary words* – teaching new words, either as they appear in text, or by introducing new words separately. This type of instruction also aids reading ability.

– *Reading comprehension strategies* – techniques for helping individuals to understand what they read. Such techniques involve having students summarize what they've read, to gain a better understanding of the material'.

In the full report, the Panel claimed that '[t]he results of the meta-analysis were impressive. Overall, the findings showed that teaching children to manipulate phonemes in words was highly effective under a variety of teaching conditions with a variety of learners across a range of grade and age levels and that teaching phonemic awareness to children significantly improves their reading more than instruction that lacks any attention to [phonemic awareness]' (National Reading Panel, 2000, 2.2). This is considered to be one of the biggest and most important findings in reading research over the past 50 years. (Note that comparison is made with 'instruction that lacks any attention to [phonemic awareness]' and that no reference is made to the *amount* of attention devoted to phonemic awareness.) But is this knowledge really all that new?

State of the art in 1908

In 1908, Professor Edmund Burke Huey published a book entitled *The Psychology and Pedagogy of Reading. With a Review of the History of Reading and Writing and of Methods, Texts, and Hygiene in Reading*. This probably is the first overview of research in the field – and as it turns out, even then people were already discussing the importance of phonemes, phonemic awareness and Phonics.

> The phonic method used by the Jansenists in the Port Royal Schools, long neglected but advocated again by Thornton in 1790, began, as we have seen, to be extensively used as a special method in this country in the system of Leigh, about 1870–1873. It is a spelling method, but the word is spelled by its elementary sounds and not by the letter-names. The word is slowly pronounced until its constituent sounds come to consciousness, and these sounds are associated with the letters representing them. Drill in this sound analysis trains the articulation, trains the ear and the ability to sound the letters of any new word and gives the power to pronounce it by blending the sounds [...]. (Huey, 1908, p. 266)

In this connection, there began a debate against the background of the fact that the English language has more sounds than it has letters. Some people claimed that '[t]he forty-four or more sounds used in English needed as many characters, and when these were furnished the method came to be known as the phonetic, to distinguish it from the simpler phonic' (p. 267).

Huey is convinced that children must learn to break printed or handwritten words down into letters and that they must learn to associate those letters with sounds. Further, they must also learn to make syntheses of those sounds. And the wholes thus arrived at, they must learn to associate with words of spoken language. However, the key questions in this context are when children are to learn these things, and how they should learn them. Huey stresses repeatedly that two circumstances must be taken into account in learning to decode words in the above-mentioned way: first, that the oral stream of speech is continuous, meaning that it may be difficult for children to isolate its component elements; and second, that the child's natural unit is semantic in nature. Specifically, some people claimed that the smallest semantic unit is the sentence, because it reproduces an idea, while others considered that children first learn the meaning of individual words – especially those corresponding to concrete objects – and that entire ideas or sentences represent a higher level of complexity.

Huey does not present any statistics on the most widely used methods in the United States in the late 19th and early 20th century, but his impression is that most teachers tend to begin their reading instruction by introducing whole sentences or whole words. Where teachers start with whole sentences, these tend to deal with topics that the children have experienced and are interested in. For example, a lesson may begin with a type of ball game. When the children are holding the ball, they say, 'I am holding a ball'. That sentence is then written on the blackboard, or is already printed in a book. Each time the children see the sentence, they are reminded of the situation or experience to which it refers. After some time, the written images begin to be analysed: 'the sentence-wholes are gradually analyzed into their constituent words and these again, in time, into their constituent sounds and letters. The important thing is to begin with meaning wholes [...] letting analysis follow in its own time' (p. 274). However, methods of a type that we today associate with Phonics also existed back then:

> Of these the 'Synthetic Method of Reading and Spelling', by Rebecca S. Pollard, has been very widely used, although its popularity is waning. This method is purely phonic, almost arrogantly so. The author states that 'there must be no guesswork, no reference to pictures, no waiting for a story from the teacher to develop the thought' [...] The main business of the method is to make the child able to pronounce words for himself as he comes to them in reading new matter, and it accomplishes this result pretty effectually. (p. 281)

Huey's main objection to Phonics is that '[i]f this method is used too soon, it results in word reading, as it takes so long to get the word that the thought is lost' (p. 294). In today's terminology, we would say that the children focus on the decoding and pronunciation of individual words rather than on the meaning and coherence of the text. According to a well-known claim by Gough and Tunmer (1986), reading = decoding × comprehension. Huey may not have used that terminology nor that formula, but he would agree that correct decoding and pronunciation alone do not amount to reading. The decoding of non-words is thus not reading and should therefore not be as prominent as it is today in contexts such as the training and testing of dyslexics. Further, Huey may not have used the term 'dual route', but he did distinguish between the two alternatives involved: either the reader knows the whole word and associates directly to its meaning, or the reader has to decode the word by sounding it out (at least mentally) letter by letter. In this context, Huey warns of '[t]he danger of reading words rather than ideas' (p. 296). The most important goal, in his opinion, is to find meaning in the text, and this requires a certain amount of fluency. The joy of reading good literature is important on both counts: 'Methods come and go, but all lack the essentials of any well-grounded method, viz. relevancy to the child's mental needs' (p. 305).

To sum up, it may well be claimed that, one hundred years and more than one hundred thousand research projects later, little has changed when it comes to the goal of reading. There is a consensus that children should read texts that are as meaningful as possible to them and that they should read with fluency. There is no dispute about the importance of the desire to read. Further, there is general agreement that children need to learn how to decode and hence to learn about phonemes – while it is true that there is some difference of opinion as regards when and how children should be taught about them, Huey would claim that this is something that must be adapted to the needs of each individual child.

In the light of this, there seems to be good reason to conclude that the heated debate between Whole Language and Phonics has been very much beside the point, and of limited value. For some of the participants in that debate, considerations of prestige and power may have outweighed any concern for the children's best interests or for scientific truth. In my opinion, Michael Pressley has taken a sensible position with his 'balanced view' (cf. Pressley, 2006), but I still consider that too much attention is often devoted to determining the appropriate *proportions* or the appropriate importance to be assigned to each of these two approaches. In my opinion, it should instead be emphasised that the entire reading process constitutes a shifting back and forth between the whole and the parts, and in this context I believe that hermeneutics should be given a more prominent role (cf., e.g., Gadamer, 1960). It is in the nature of the human being to search for meaning. All sensory impressions must be interpreted, and this is done by seeing the parts in relation to the whole. When the inscription on the Rosetta Stone was first interpreted, the scholars started from an assumption about when and where the text came into being, what its purpose was, etc. On this basis, they tried to assign meaning to the individual characters. Their interpretation of the characters then altered their overall view of the text in some respects, and their new view shed new light on the interpretation of the characters. The new understanding of the characters formed the basis of a new overall view, and so on. This is called the hermeneutic circle or spiral; you never know whether you have attained a complete and correct understanding of something. The same approach is taken to read unclear and unfamiliar handwriting – and in fact also to read printed text, even though people tend not to be aware of this because familiarity with the printed characters has made the process automatic and rapid. It is more obvious that this approach is used to interpret words and sentences.

Against the background of the above, I would like to claim that reading is primarily an *interpretive skill*. Given that you never know whether you have attained a complete and correct comprehension, I consider it better to talk about 'interpretation' than 'comprehension' in reading research. This change in terminology would also entail a shift in focus, from the product to the process. When it comes to psychological schools of thought, I am of the opinion that connectionism is best able to embrace these ideas. The processes involved are not primarily sequential in nature, but rather parallel and multidirectional (cf. the connectionist concept of 'back propagation'). There is a progressive 'calibration' or closing-in on the truth, and there is a dynamic relationship between the whole and the parts. What is more, much more weight is assigned to learning, individual differences and individual change than in the cognitive school of psychology. To illustrate the relationship between the whole and the parts, I would like to refer to the following quotation from the connectionist David Rumelhart:

> I use the term perception rather freely here. In general, it is my opinion that the distinction between the perceptual and conceptual aspects of reading is not that useful. As I will suggest later, there appears to be a continuity between what has been called perception and what has been called comprehension. My use of the term perception in the present context is simply the use of the one term to cover the entire process. (Rumelhart, 1994, p. 893)

Both hermeneutics and connectionism are genuine intellectual creations of the 20th century, and I would like to claim that, applied to the study object of reading in the manner outlined in this book, they represent a mindset that deserves to be referred to as new.

IS THERE ANY EMPIRICAL RESEARCH ATTESTING TO THE IMPORTANCE OF PHONEMIC AWARENESS?

I am thus of the opinion that phonemic awareness is an absolutely central component of reading skill – but does this represent a major empirical finding? First, we have seen that even Huey stressed the importance of phonemic awareness, and he did not have as much empirical research to underpin that statement as exists today. In a sense, it can be claimed that what we are dealing with is an analytic truth which follows from the very definition of 'reading' chosen. It is commonly claimed, by reference to Gough and Tunmer (1986), that reading = decoding × comprehension. There are many definitions of 'decoding', but let us focus here on the fact that it entails a 'translation' from writing to speech. With our alphabetic system, this means that each letter (grapheme) must be associated with a sound (phoneme). In other words, decoding *requires* the ability to distinguish and identify the individual phonemes in the oral stream of speech. Hence, phonemic awareness is necessary by definition. Further, given that a 'translation' is to be made from speech, vision is also a *necessary* condition for decoding, and there are additional conditions that are necessary by definition.

A student of the history of reading and dyslexia research easily forms the impression that phonemic awareness is paramount. However, meta-studies – including those presented by the US National Reading Panel – actually show its importance to be limited. Now, why does phonology not explain more than it does? In fact, based on the definition of 'decoding', as discussed above, all we are able to say is that having phonemic skills is a necessary, but *not sufficient*, condition for reading skill (given that there are other conditions that must also be met, such as having adequate eyesight). Let me illustrate this logical difference with an example. If we define 'bachelor' as 'unmarried man', this means that both the property of 'unmarriedness' and the property of 'manhood' are necessary in order for the term 'bachelor' to be used. On its own, neither of these properties is logically sufficient, but together they constitute a necessary *and sufficient* condition for using the term 'bachelor'. In other words, 'bachelor' can be used *if and only if* a person is both a man and unmarried.

As regards the empirical part of the research, I would like to add that the vast majority of studies show that phonemic awareness is indeed required for learning to read. It is also clear that those who have the opportunity to practise phonemic skills will perform better at tests later on. But what kind of tests are those? As a rule, they are decoding tests where the key variables are the number of mistakes and the rate of decoding. Using the above-mentioned definition, this means that the skills measured are largely identical to the skills practised, and it is hardly surprising that practising phonemic skills will cause students to perform measurably better at those same skills. Further, the fact that phonemic awareness is a necessary condition does not have to entail that improvement to those skills will always result in a corresponding increase in the rate of decoding – there might well be a threshold value beyond which an improvement in phonemic skills will not cause decoding skills to improve correspondingly.

Analogous conclusions can be drawn as regards dyslexia. If we claim that phonemic awareness is necessary for decoding, this means that inadequate phonemic awareness is logically *sufficient* to cause decoding problems – which are commonly defined as 'dyslexia'. When it comes to empirical studies, there is reason to emphasise a problem that I have already dealt with in an article entitled 'How can we best define "dyslexia"?' (Tønnessen, 1997a), namely that 'phonemic difficulties' are often included in the definition of 'dyslexia'. When a dyslexia group is to be selected for a research project, care is typically taken to ensure that its members, but not those of the control group, have phonemic difficulties. Then it is only natural that the prevalence of phonemic difficulties will be higher among dyslexics! In other words, the conclusion that phonemes and phonemic awareness are important factors in both reading skill and dyslexia is one that follows from the fundamental definitions used. What is more, most studies have only tested the null hypothesis and reported p values, which means that they are of limited value. Fortunately, the calculation of effect size has gained an increasingly prominent place.

Regardless of the fact that many new ideas about the importance of phonemes in reading are not empirical but logical-analytic in nature, they do represent useful clarifications and reminders. However, additional reflection at the level of the philosophy of science would contribute towards assigning appropriate places to those insights as well as towards the search for (new) empirical questions to be asked.

Even though the concepts of 'phoneme', 'phonemic awareness', 'phonology' and 'Phonics' have had a very central place in reading and dyslexia research, fundamental questions in this context have been explored only to a relatively small extent. The level of precision should have been higher and a series of philosophical problems should have been clarified. In this field, Uppstad (2005) has made important contributions.

HAS COGNITIVE PSYCHOLOGY BEEN BENEFICIAL TO READING RESEARCH?

Psychology was dominated by behaviourism from the 1930s to the 1960s. After that, it was cognitive psychology that exerted a dominant influence, during a period also characterised by a large increase in reading and dyslexia research, which largely chose cognitive methods. It is open to discussion both for how long this cognitive dominance lasted and how it manifested itself, but even so I consider that cognitive psychology has left such deep marks in reading and dyslexia research that special attention should be devoted to it. I will focus particularly on a number of problems and limitations associated with that school of psychology. This means that I will address themes that deserve to be treated far more thoroughly than it is possible to do here, but I hope that I will be able to contribute towards further reflections. Howard Gardner makes use of the term 'cognitive revolution' (Gardner, 1985). In science, 'revolution' is above all associated with Thomas Kuhn's theory of science (Kuhn, 1970), where a revolution involves shifts in the paradigms of research, including radical changes in fundamental methods and ways of thinking. One example is the shift from Newtonian to Einsteinian physics. The move from behaviourism to cognitive psychology is hardly comparable to that major change in physics. It is also clear that cognitive psychology has many precursors in both psychology and philosophy. One example is gestalt psychology, in relation to which Hergenhahn (1992) noted that '[p]resent-day cognitive psychology – with its emphasis on organization, structure, relationships, the active role of the subject, and the important part played by perception in learning and memory – reflects the influence of its Gestalt antecedents' (p. 544). In the field of philosophy, the obvious precursors include Plato and Descartes.

What is more, it is often unclear what the concept of 'cognition' includes. Hergenhahn (1992) claims that cognitive psychology deals primarily with 'language, thinking, perception, problem solving, concept formation, memory, learning, intelligence, and attention' (p. 543). Hence, irrational phenomena such as needs, emotions, wishes, interests, motivation, faith, imagination, creativity, etc., are out of reach of cognitive psychology – as originally delimited. Rationalist philosophy, which inspired cognitive psychology, also took no interest in those phenomena and had no place for them. When individual thinkers have subsequently attempted to extend the concept of 'cognition', they have ended up at odds both with the tradition and with their own foundations. Gardner (1985) claims that '[c]ognitive science is predicated on the belief that it is legitimate – in fact necessary – to posit a separate level of analysis which can be called the "level of representation". When working at this level, a scientist traffics in such representational entities as symbols, rules, images – the stuff of representation which is found between input and output – and in addition, explores the ways in which these representational entities are joined, transformed, or contrasted with one another' (p. 38).

While behaviourism talked about a 'black box' between stimulus and response, cognitive psychology thus wishes to explore the inner life, which cannot be observed from the outside. Instead of 'stimulus' and 'response', they use the terms 'input' and 'output', which they have borrowed from computer science. This is no coincidence: according to Gardner (1987), 'not all cognitive scientists make the computer central to their daily work, [but] nearly all have been strongly influenced by it' (p. 40). Hergenhahn (1992) stresses that '[t]here is no better example of how developments outside psychology can influence psychology than the emergence of information-processing cognitive psychology. Most information processing psychologists note the similarities between humans and computers [...]' (p. 543). The brain is commonly compared to a computer and thoughts to software. What takes place between input and output is called 'processing', a word originally borrowed from chemistry and biology but now also established in the field of computer science. Cognitive psychology tries to find the most adequate way possible to break a process down into sub-processes or sub-tasks, which are often presented in the form of flowcharts. In the case of reading, one possible such breakdown is as follows: First, two options or routes are distinguished: (1) the direct route, where the reader recognises the word as a whole and is able to move directly from written image to meaning; and (2) the indirect route, which readers use when they do not recognise the whole word. This second route yields the following sub-processes or sub-tasks: (a) visual analysis of the written image; (b) isolation and identification of each letter, in the order as written; (c) association of each letter with the corresponding sound; (d) linking together of those sounds; (e) pronunciation of the whole; and (f) association of that whole with a word of spoken language. (A typical example of how reading is treated in cognitive psychology can be found in Ellis (1993).) The main contribution of cognitive psychology concerns the description of the reading process; it has been less useful when it comes to explaining or understanding that process.

Now, do these flowcharts represent an empirical finding? In my opinion, their main function is to make the ramifications of the definition of 'reading' more precise. The various sub-tasks cannot be identified unless it has first been defined what reading is. However, empirical studies can provide information about the relative order of the sub-tasks and about ways of distinguishing between them. For example, there are studies showing that some people are able to associate each letter with the corresponding sound (sub-task 2 c) but not to link those sounds together (sub-task 2 d). This allows the conclusion that these are two distinct tasks. In the case of linking the sounds together (sub-task 2 d) and pronouncing the whole (sub-task 2 e), however, it can be questioned whether someone has really linked the sounds together if he or she is unable to pronounce the resultant whole; this is largely a matter of definitions. Since the breakdown into sub-tasks largely follows from the definition, all such flowcharts have something normative about them: they show how it is deemed that reading should be done, or what is a normal reading process. According to Hergenhahn (1992), '[t]he information-processing psychologist usually concentrates his or her research on normal, rational thinking and behavior and views the human as an active seeker and user of information' (p. 543). In the diagnosis of reading difficulties, it is important to know which sub-tasks are causing problems, because this makes it possible to engage in special practice of those sub-tasks. However, this is easier to do with some sub-tasks than with others. For example, there are a number of potential reasons why students may have difficulties associating a sound package with a word of spoken language. If, say, the sounds /s/+/ʌ/+/n/ are pronounced too slowly, it may be difficult to associate the whole with the familiar word 'sun' of spoken language. The same is true if a word is incorrectly stressed. Gardner (1985) further claims that, '[t]hough mainstream cognitive scientists do not necessarily bear any animus against the affective realm, against the context that surrounds any action or thought, or against historical or cultural analyses, in practice they attempt to factor out these elements to the maximum extent possible' (p. 41). In other words, emotions, needs, punishment and reward, which were absolutely central to behaviourism, have little

101

place in the descriptions and explanations provided by cognitive psychology. However, if biological needs and feelings are not included, the best that can be hoped for is to find reasons; causes will be completely out of reach. It is hard to imagine how thoughts alone could be the driver of human actions. People cannot prioritise among their thoughts unless there are habits or emotions associated with them. This means that both motivation and learning are difficult to explain in cognitive psychology. Indeed, Bechtel and Abrahamsen (1991) assert that '[c]ognitive psychologists and artificial intelligence researchers [...] tended to ignore learning until recently' (p. 69). What cognitive psychology primarily shows is how input is processed and transformed into output. It does not show how humans learn. According to Thorne and Henley (2001), '[r]ule-based systems have limits, and one of [artificial intelligence]'s remaining problems is that humans gain new knowledge by learning, something most computers do not do, and something neglected by most cognitive psychologists' (p. 549).

Cognitive psychology may not have accounted for principles of learning in its theory, but in its practice it has used such principles – mainly borrowed from behaviourism. For example, the association of graphemes with phonemes requires many repetitions, leading to strong associations and automatisation. But when it comes to why people move in a specific order from sub-task to sub-task in the flowchart, it is necessary to ask whether this is really also due to association and automatisation, or whether it might have something to do with the goal pulling 'from the end': the wish to find meaning. (According to Hergenhahn (1992), many cognitive psychologists actually claim that the human being is an 'active seeker [...] of information' (p. 543). That claim presupposes the existence of irrational interests, which are outside the tradition of cognitivism.) Such an explanation would be teleological rather than causal, but how could wishes be explained rationally and cognitively? The flowcharts of cognitive psychology can show what sub-tasks are creating problems in reading, but they cannot explain why someone ends up having problems with those sub-tasks. To do that, cognitivists will have to borrow causes from other fields or schools such as medicine, behaviourism or connectionism. However, the combination of those with cognitive psychology gives rise to philosophical problems that have hardly been addressed at all in research.

Can cognitive psychology be used in special-needs education to remedy reading difficulties? As mentioned above, it can point us to the location of the problems between input and output, but the classic definition of 'cognitive' mentioned by Gardner (1985) and others cannot accommodate methods such as 'over-learning', which are available to behaviourism. My interpretation of this is that from the 1980s, cognitive psychology increasingly looked for solutions in two fields: metacognition and neurology.

Metacognition is consistent with the fundamental principles of cognitive psychology. It uses cognition to solve cognitive problems. However, this solution gives rise to many problems. At the philosophical level, it is controversial what metacognition means and whether it is possible: Can we really be aware of our awareness? Is this not as difficult as seeing our eye while seeing? At the scientific level, metacognition is problematic because it seems to require introspection, which cannot be either verified or falsified. At the educational level, finally, metacognition could perhaps be said to be about learning to learn – but this is a very abstract and demanding notion, especially to those with learning difficulties.

If neurology is brought in, there arises a philosophical question about the relationship between the mental and the physical. One solution is reductionism. However, that would mean that the problems are not really cognitive, but medical – and so cognitivism would give up trying to solve the problems on the basis of its own principles.

WHAT KIND OF A PHENOMENON IS READING?

When I started working in the field of reading and dyslexia research twenty-five years ago, the first question I asked myself was: What kind of phenomenon am I going to investigate? It may seem odd to begin a career in empirical research with so theoretical issues, but the big differences between how cognitive psychology and behaviourism view the goals and methods of research make it clear that theoretical opinions may have a large practical impact.

I drew inspiration from Aristotle (384–322 B.C.). In his exploration of the human being, he was flanked on one side by Plato (428–348 B.C.), who placed all emphasis on ideas and on the rational, and on the other side by materialists such as Democritus (460–370 B.C.). Present-day psychology is in a similar situation, with cognitivism and behaviourism on either side. In my opinion, the former school commits an intellectualistic fallacy while the latter commits a mechanistic fallacy. I think Aristotle offered a good combination of theory and practice, which he often illustrated with examples from the world of craftsmen and artists: 'For the things we have to learn before we can do them, we learn by doing them, e.g. men become builders by building and lyreplayers by playing the lyre; so too we become just by doing just acts, temperate by doing temperate acts, brave by doing brave acts' (*Nichomachean Ethics*, Book II, 1). In this context, Aristotle also makes an important distinction between potentiality and the realisation of potentials. Heraclitus (540–480 B.C.) claimed that everything is in constant change. Plato's view, by contrast, was that anything that truly exists is unchangeable. Aristotle's position was that when for example a human being develops, there is something that remains constant and something that changes: there is both continuity and discontinuity between childhood and old age. The distinction between potentiality and realisation has been very important throughout history when it comes to explaining change. In psychology and linguistics, for example, we see today how Noam Chomsky assumes a version of Plato's position – or, to be precise, of Descartes's position. Chomsky believes that all humans are born with the same linguistic structures. These do not change, but humans discover and use them to a greater or lesser extent. According to Aristotle's way of thinking, this leaves no room for genuine change and development. Inspired by Aristotle, I thought this might be the place to find a key to a fruitful combination of behaviourism and cognitive psychology. I found that Aristotle's examples and terminology best corresponded to the concept of 'skill'. The combination of theory and practice (and of mind and body) inherent in that concept is extremely important in all human activity, but it has been clarified and deepened only to a limited extent. In everyday language, the word 'skill' tends to be used mainly about physical or motor tasks that require automatisation, mechanical drill and habituation. However, I would like to emphasise that this needs to be combined with conscious monitoring and control. It should thus be possible to obtain important elements for my combination endeavour from both behaviourism and cognitive psychology.

What is important is finding the right combination and alternation between automaticity and awareness. If, say, a cyclist trusts his 'autopilot' too much, unexpected situations may give rise to big problems. But devoting too much attention to keeping one's balance may also cause big problems. The key is adjusting the use of automaticity and awareness, respectively, to circumstances. In other words, there must be a flexible and situationally determined alternation between the two.

When it comes to the relationship between reading, dyslexia and automatisation, I was first inspired by Nicolson and Fawcett (1990), who found that dyslexics did not only have automatisation problems in the actual reading process, which had been noted before, but also problems in motor processes, including balance. On this basis, they claimed that 'dyslexic children will suffer problems in fluency for any skill that should become automatic through extensive practice' (Nicolson & Fawcett, 1990, p. 29) and developed what has been referred to as the 'dyslexic automatisation deficit hypothesis'. This has later been supplemented with the 'conscious compensation hypothesis', which states that, 'despite their more limited automaticity of skill, dyslexic children are able to perform at apparently normal levels most of the time by "consciously compensating", that is, by consciously concentrating (controlled processing) on performance that would normally be automatic' (Nicolson & Fawcett, 2010, p. 68ff). Here they come close to my own ideas about awareness. One way in which they tested their hypothesis was to make dyslexics perform several tasks at the same time, which they turned out to be much worse at than normal readers. I will not go into detail about the hypotheses and the testing of them, but they provided a great deal of stimulus for my work. However, while Nicolson and Fawcett stress automaticity, I consider that the problem, or the challenge, is to find a flexible and appropriate alternation between automaticity and awareness. This is in fact what I define as the characteristic common to all skills. Most people who discuss skills – including Nicolson and Fawcett – focus too much on automaticity. When it comes to awareness, it is important to distinguish two aspects: seeing and noticing. Someone riding a bike will see everything on the road and in the surrounding landscape, but she will not notice everything. A reader sees the whole text but does not notice all details.

LaBerge and Samuels (1974) claim that automatisation in reading is particularly important to free the maximum amount of resources for the task of finding the meaning of a text. In their opinion, automatisation primarily encompasses the most elementary tasks, such as processing of visual information, perception, identification of letters and sounds, linking together of sounds, etc. In my view, by contrast, comprehension – or, rather: interpretation – must also be automatised, at the same time as awareness must also be used. As already mentioned, I see reading primarily as an interpretive process, from the interpretation of letters to the interpretation of entire texts. This interpretation process is based on constantly seeing wholes and parts in relation to each other, and this hermeneutic alternation between wholes and parts is a skill which must combine awareness and automaticity in a flexible manner. I thus started by asking questions about what kind of phenomenon reading is. As mentioned, I have found it to be mainly a skill. To a lesser degree, however, it is also knowledge, for example knowledge about the relationships between graphemes and phonemes or about the meaning of words. Reading shares the quality of being a skill with many other human activities. What, then, is the difference between reading and other skills such as swimming or cycling? One of the most specific sub-skills involved in reading is interpretation, and this, in turn, consists of various sub-skills. For example, readers interpret written characters as well as the meaning of words and sentences. All of this requires automaticity and awareness. Other important sub-skills include making associations between graphemes and phonemes, and synthesising sounds into whole sound packages to be associated with meanings in spoken language. This must be automatised, but it must also be made subject to awareness.

Dreyfus and Dreyfus (1990) claim that people first learn a skill by following rules. After a while they will perform the skill automatically, without thinking. This automatic performance may become mechanical, so the next step of development, they say, is based on intuition. In my opinion, this is obfuscation; the word 'intuition' has many definitions, and all of them are unclear. Actually, a good speed-skater or tightrope-walker does not use intuition, but rather a constant combination and alternation between automaticity and conscious monitoring and control. In the event of problems or mistakes, there is a need for active control. Such control is often based on trial and error. If, say, a cyclist finds herself in an entirely new situation, she cannot draw upon either rules or automaticity. The choice of solutions or actions in such circumstances will depend on experience, knowledge, habits and creativity. If the first attempts fail, new ones will be made. On this point, I draw inspiration from the way in which Karl Popper thinks that problems are solved in research (Popper, 1963). People learn through trial and error, but as a rule this is not explicit. Rather, it is a question of implicit learning and of tacit knowledge or skills (cf. Reber, 1993). Such learning or acquisition of skills leads to changes in the nervous system which have been well described and explained by connectionist psychology – while cognitive psychology has no help to offer on this count. Bechtel and Abrahamsen (1991) maintain that '[m]any psychologists were influenced by Chomsky as they moved from behaviorism to information processing because his grammar suggested ways to model human knowledge using linguistic-style rules' (p. 13). However, even though Chomsky has various definitions of 'rules', they all relate to norms and intentions 'up front' that 'pull' (teleological explanations) rather than causal factors 'in the back' that 'push'. For cognitivists, the order of the day is rule-following, while connectionists see things – like natural phenomena – as rule-governed, even though they prefer to talk about regularities rather than rules. One example of this is how children gradually learn irregular past-tense forms in English (cf. McClelland, Rumelhart, & the PDP Research Group, 1986): a type of trial-and-error process takes place until a stable state or equilibrium is attained, and networks are built analogously to the forming of associations in behaviourist theory. Hence connectionists do not think that people are governed by innate systems or structures, as Chomsky claims, inspired by Descartes – and Plato.

Both behaviourists and connectionists assign very great importance to learning. Chomsky distinguishes between 'competence' and 'performance'. The former is the universal grammar or set of rules followed by all languages and all thinking. It corresponds to the rules of logic that all rational thinking must follow. Performance is the practical application of the rules. This distinction to some extent evokes my own claim that a skill is a potential that can be realised in different ways. However, Chomsky is inspired by Plato's views on learning. In his dialogue Meno, Plato shows how all learning involves bringing knowledge to the surface of awareness through recollection. Socrates exemplifies this through his famous interrogation of Meno's slave, where he uses his maieutics to make the slave boy solve a geometrical problem concerning the relationship between the sides and the diagonal of a square, apparently without the boy having any previous knowledge of the matter. Learning, on this view, consists in finding out what is already inside us.

When I use the word 'potentiality' in the context of skills, I draw inspiration from Aristotle, who tried to explain change in that way. For example, water is potentially both ice and steam (see Chapter 4). The realisation of either potential entails a real change. Both the acquisition of a skill and the realisation of a skill also entail real change – this does not just amount to discovering what already exists. Realisations may vary greatly depending on the person and the situation, but this thus does not mean that people just see, more or less clearly, the correct solutions that they already have inside them. In my opinion, Aristotle's theory of potentials is better in line with empirical findings in psychology and educational science than is Plato's theory, which has inspired Chomsky and others.

I have already presented the classic version of cognitive psychology, but for the sake of clarity I would like to repeat the following characteristics: (1) inner representations (images); (2) rules or algorithms for processing those representations (inspired by computer software); and (3) sequential processing of representations, broken down into as small units as possible. This typically manifests itself in flowcharts; the best-known one in the field of reading and dyslexia research is the dual-route chart. Connectionism rejects all three of these points, starting instead from how nerves or nerve cells work. In this respect, connectionism represents a further development of behaviourism. It wishes to explain the driving forces of the human mind. In my opinion, making use of an eclectic mix of behaviourism, cognitive psychology and connectionism would give rise to many philosophical problems, but even so these three schools of psychology can work together in the description and explanation of skills. They can be seen as the three corners of a triangle, or as three sides of a mountain-top.

Nicolson and Fawcett consider that problems with automatisation are primarily attributable to anomalies in the cerebellum. However, here it is also relevant to refer to the research carried out by John Stein, who has long claimed that visual factors represent the main problem of dyslexics. After the relationship between the magnocellular and parvocellular systems had been investigated, he formed the opinion that the explanation could be an anomaly in the magnocellular system of dyslexics, claiming that '[t]he magnocellular system is known to be important for direction of visual attention and, therefore, of eye movement, hence for visual search also' (Stein, 2001, p. 19). In addition, Stein believes that the visual functions are not alone in being impaired by shortcomings in the magnocellular system, referring to corresponding findings in the auditive field and relating to tactile sensation. Stein's conclusion is that '[i]t seems therefore, that magnocells in general might be affected in dyslexics' (p. 26). As regards the relationship with the cerebellum, he asserts that '[t]hus the cerebellum not only receives timing signals from magnocellular systems in other parts of the brain, but also it can be considered itself, perhaps the most important part of the magnocellular timing system of the brain' (p. 27). Here it should be noted that the tasks of the parvocellular system are to focus on details and to check whether the quick registration of wholes carried out by the magnocellular system is correct. The magnocellular system reacts to movement and to wholes, while the parvocellular one registers details and requires concentration. In fact, the interplay between these two systems is a good fit with the interplay between the whole and the parts found in hermeneutics. It also corresponds well to the rapid reactions required for automaticity and the deeper and more concentrated efforts required for awareness. These are hypotheses that may be worthy of further development and deepening. Among other things, they could indicate that the relatively common double-deficit theory or hypothesis – where a distinction is made between problems with phonological processing and problems with rapid automatised naming (RAN) (cf. Wolf & Bowers, 1999) – can be reduced to underlying shortcomings in automaticity and awareness (compare also Nicolson & Fawcett, 2010, pp. 25–28).

I would also like to mention the research carried out by Dirk Bakker (1990), who claims that there are two types of dyslexia: the 'P' type associated with the right hemisphere of the brain, which sees wholes; and the 'L' type associated with the left hemisphere, which sees details. This corresponds to the alternation between the whole and the parts seen in hermeneutics, and also to the alternation between quick hypotheses (automaticity) and monitoring, verification and falsification (awareness).

WHAT FOUNDATION SHOULD WE BUILD ON?

Frith (1997) distinguishes four levels in reading and dyslexia research: (1) the biological level; (2) the psychological level; (3) the behavioural level; and (4) the environmental level. While this is a good simplification for educational purposes, what is needed in a scientific context is an extensive clarification of each level as well as an analysis and explanation of the differences and relationships between them (see Chapter 2). These distinctions give rise to many philosophical problems that we cannot deal with here; one of them, though, caused by the distinction between levels 1 and 2, is the classic body–mind problem. Behaviourism was highly materialist and positivist in nature, preferring to concern itself only with phenomena that can be observed using the senses. Cognitive psychology wanted to include mental and subjective circumstances as well. Connectionism wished to take knowledge about the workings of nerves as its primary starting point, meaning that in this respect it was closer to behaviourism than to cognitivism. At the same time, however, it did not want to restrict itself to the 'black-box psychology' of behaviourism. Rather, like cognitive psychology, it wished to describe and explain inner phenomena, but without recourse to the inner representations of cognitivism. Connectionists considered there to be no grounds for making a sharp distinction between the body and the mind. It is open to discussion whether this amounted to neglecting or blurring an important problem. Personally, I think that the body and the mind should be distinguished, but not separated. Humans have a body that others can observe, but we also have mental states that others cannot observe. These two form a unit and a whole, but phenomena in one area cannot be fully explained by means of phenomena from the other (reductionism). Rather, their inter-relationship can be compared to two sides of the same mountain-top. They come across as different but belong together. And yet they are not each other's causes.

Through our senses, we are influenced by both social and cultural phenomena. Some people have claimed that there is an opposition between psychological and socio-cultural studies of reading, but I think that is an artificial opposition. It is obvious that the literary works and the language that we read are socio-cultural phenomena, but the reading as such and the search for meaning must be carried out by individuals. The interpretive process involved is a psychological phenomenon, but what is being interpreted are socio-cultural phenomena.

The four levels of Frith's model have a parallel in the flowcharts so beloved of cognitive psychology, with their clearly defined sub-tasks carried out in a specified order. This is a mechanistic way of thinking, inspired among other things by the architecture and working procedures of computers. Such analyses have traditionally been characterised as 'homuncular' because they give the impression that there is a series of internal 'units' that perform the various tasks in an autonomous fashion. One of the most influential researchers when it comes to modules and faculties in cognitive psychology is Fodor (1983), but others' support for his ideas has progressively become less widespread and more nuanced. However, this way of thinking has left many traces in cognitive psychology that remain to this day. To the extent that connectionism illustrates inner processes, it does not represent them as clearly delimited, sequentially ordered 'boxes'. The individual components are bigger and less clearly delimited, and the processes are parallel (hence connectionism's alternative name of 'parallel distributed processing') rather than just sequential, multidirectional rather than unidirectional.

Connectionism takes a more vitalist than mechanist view in this respect. Its ideas are more inspired by living organisms than by mechanical instruments. The whole is not just the sum of the parts. Further, the goal of each activity is for the entire system to attain stability or balance. To some extent, this way of thinking can therefore be characterised as teleological. Cybernetic ideas may come even closer, with a constant interplay between the whole and the parts. And this way of thinking also has much in common with the one I have mentioned in relation to hermeneutics: the interpretive process will always involve seeing the whole and the parts in the light of each other, and the process will continue for as long as there is a discordance between the parts and the whole. In a sense, this is a version of the hypothetico-deductive method, where hypotheses and empirical data mutually adjust each other (Føllesdal, 1979).

It is open to discussion whether, and in what sense or to what extent, cognitive psychology is based on teleological 'explanations'. Aristotle's distinction between goals that 'pull' (teleologically) and causes that 'push' (causally) has progressively become less pronounced. For example, cybernetics has contributed to their unification. In addition, it can be claimed that Karl Popper's ideas, which are inspired by Darwinism, help to blur the line between the teleological and the causal. According to Popper, people solving problems – especially scientific ones – tend to build on spontaneity and creativity to a large extent. This corresponds to mutations in Darwin's evolutionary theory: if ideas do not 'collide' with empirical data, they 'survive'. In retrospect, it may seem that developments in a scientific field have had a goal (been teleological), but spontaneous and creative experiments or hypotheses are usually not the product of necessity or chance. They represent a combination that we do not yet have a good name for.

We need to search for new paradigms and hypotheses in order to make further progress in reading and dyslexia research. In the past forty years, cognitive psychology has become too dominant. In my opinion, that school of psychology must be combined with behaviourism and connectionism – but not eclectically, through more or less random choice of elements from each of these three schools. One way of doing this is by conceiving of reading as an interpretive or hermeneutic skill which can be described or studied from three different sides – similarly to how it is possible to approach a mountain-top from three sides. However, a number of theoretical and philosophical issues must be clarified in order for this to be possible. This book is intended as a contribution to those clarification efforts.

REFERENCES

Aaron, P. G. (1989). *Dyslexia and hyperlexia*. Dordrecht: Kluwer.

Aaron, P. G., & Joshi, R. M. (1992). *Reading problems: Consultation and remediation*. New York: Guilford Press.

Adams, M. J., Stahl, S. A., Osborne, J., & Lehr, F. (1990). *Beginning to read: The new phonics in context*. Heinemann Educational.

Adams, M. J. (1990). *Beginning to read. Thinking and learning about print*. Cambridge, MA: MIT Press.

Adams, M. J. (1994). Modeling the connections between word recognition and reading. In R. B. Ruddell, M. R. Ruddell, & H. Singer (Eds.), *Theoretical models and processes of reading* (4th edition). Newark: International Reading Association.

Allington, R. L. (1983). Fluency: The neglected reading goal. *The Reading Teacher, 36*, 556–561.

Altwerger, B., Jordan, N., & Shelton, N.R. (2007). *Reading fluency: Process, practice, and policy*. Portsmouth, NH: Heinemann.

American Psychiatric Association. (1987). *Diagnostic and statistical manual of mental disorders* (DSM-III-R). Washington, DC: American Psychiatric Association.

Anderson, R. C., Hiebert, E. H., Scott, J. A., & Wilkinson, I. A. G. (1985). *Becoming a nation of readers: The report of the Commission on Reading*. Washington, DC: National Institute of Education.

Aristotle. (1934). *The Nicomachean ethics* (H. Rackham, Transl.). Cambridge, MA: Harvard University Press.

Ausubel, D. (1968). *Educational psychology: A cognitive view*. New York: Holt, Rinehart, and Winston.

Baars, B. J. (1986). *The cognitive revolution in psychology*. New York: Guilford Press.

Bakker, D. J. (1990a). *Developmental dyslexia and learning disorders: Diagnosis and treatment*. Michigan: Karger.

Bakker, D. J. (1990b). *Neuropsychological treatment of dyslexia*. Oxford: Oxford University Press.

Bannatyne, A. (1971). *Language, reading and learning disabilities*. Springfield: Charles C.

Battig, W. (1975). Within-individual differences in' cognitive' processes. In R. L. Solso (Ed.), *Information processing and cognition* (pp. 195–228). Hillsdale, NJ: Erlbaum.

Baum, W. M. (2005). *Understanding behaviorism: Behavior, Culture and Evolution*. Oxford: Blackwell.

Bechtel, W. (1988). *Philosophy of mind: An overview for cognitive science*. Hillsdale, NJ: Erlbaum.

Bechtel, W., & Abrahamson, A. (1991). *Connectionism and the mind: An introduction to parallel processing in networks*. London: Blackwell.

Berlin, B., & Kay, P. (1969). *Basic color terms: Their universality and evolution*. Berkeley, CA: University of California Press.

Berninger, V. W., & Abbott, R. D. (1994). Redefining learning disabilities: moving beyond IQ-achievement discrepancies to failure to respond to validated treatment protocols. In G. R. Lyon (Ed.), *Frames of reference for the assessment of learning disabilities: New views on measurement issues*. Baltimore, MD: Paul H. Brookes.

Blachman, B. A. (1997). Early intervention and phonological awareness: A cautionary tale. In B. A. Blachman (Ed.), *Foundations of reading acquisition and dyslexia: Implications for early intervention* (pp. 409–430). Mahwah, NJ: Erlbaum.

Boder, E. (1973). Developmental dyslexia: A diagnostic approach based on three atypical reading patterns. *Developmental Medicine and Child Neurology, 15*, 663–687.

Bolles, R. C. (1983). The explanation of behavior. *The Psychological Record, 33*, 31–48.

Bond, G. I., & Dykstra, R. (1967). The cooperative research program in first-grade reading instruction. *Reading Research Quarterly, 2*, 5–142.

REFERENCES

Bradley, L., & Bryant, P. E. (1983). Categorizing sounds and learning to read – a causal connection. *Nature*, *303*, 419–421.
Brady, S. A., & Shankweiler, D. (1991). *Phonological processes in literacy: A tribute to Isabelle Y. Liberman*. Hillsdale, NJ: Lawrence Erlbaum Associates.
Brady, S. A., Shankweiler, D., & Mann, V. (1983). Speech perception and memory coding in relation to reading ability. *Journal of Experimental Child Psychology*, *35*, 345–367.
Breznitz, Z., Shaul, S., Horowitz-Kraus, T., Sela, I., Nevat, M., & Karni, A. (2013). Enhanced reading by training with imposed time constraint in typical and dyslexic adults. *Nature Communications*, *4*.
Brook, A., & Mandik, P. (2004). The Philosophy of neuroscience movement. *Analyse & Kritik*, *26*, 382–397.
Brumbaugh, R. S. (1977). *The world's most mysterious manuscript*. London: Weidenfeld & Nicolson.
Cardon, L. R., Smith, S. D., Fulker, D. W., Kimberling, B. F., Pennington, B. F., & DeFries, J .C. (1994). Quantitative trait locus for reading disability on chromosome 6. *Science*, *226*, 276–279.
Chall, J. (1967). *Learning to read: The great debate*. New York: McGraw-Hill.
Chard, D. J., Pikulski, J. J., & McDonagh, S. (2006). Fluency: The link between decoding and comprehension for struggling readers. In T. Rasinski, C. Blachowicz, & K. Lems (Eds.). *Teaching reading fluency* (pp. 39–61). New York: Guilford Press.
Chomsky, N. (1957). *Syntactic structures*. The Hague/Paris: Mouton.
Chomsky, N. (1966). *Cartesian linguistics: A chapter in the history of rationalist thought*. New York: Harper & Row.
Chomsky, N. (2006). *Language and the mind.* Cambridge: Cambridge University Press.
Cohen, D. (1977). *Psychologists on psychology*. New York: Taplinger.
Coltheart, M. (1978). Lexical access in simple reading tasks. In G. Underwood (Ed.), *Strategies of information processing* (pp. 151–216). London: Academic Press.
Coltheart, M. (2005). Modeling reading: The dual-route approach. In M. J. Snowling & C. Hulme (Eds.), *The science of reading. A handbook* (pp. 6–23). Oxford: Blackwell Publishing.
Coltheart, M. (2006). Dual route and connectionist models of reading: An overview. *London Review of Education*, *4*(1), 5–17.
Coltheart, M., Curtis, B., Atkins, P., & Haller, M. (1993). Models of reading aloud: Dualroute and parallel-distributed-processing approaches. *Psychological Review*, *100*, 589–608.
Cowen, J. E. (2003). *A balanced approach to beginning reading instruction*. Newark: International Reading Association.
Critchley, M. (1964). *Developmental dyslexia*. London: William Heinemann Medical Books Limited.
Critchley, M. (1970). *The dyslexic child*. Springfield, IL: Charles C. Thomas.
Critchley, M., & Critchley, E. (1978). *Dyslexia defined*. London: Heinemann Medical Books.
DeFries, J. C., Filipek, P. A., Fulker, D. W., Olson, R. K., Pennington, B. F., Smith, S. D., & Wise, B. W. (1997). Colorado Learning Disabilities Research Center. *Learning Disabilities: A Multidisciplinary Journal*, *8*, 7–19.
de Jong, P. F., & van der Leij, A. (1999). Specific contributions of phonological abilities to early reading acquisition: Results from a Dutch latent variable longitudinal study. *Journal of Educational Psychology*, *91*, 450–476.
Denckla, M. B., & Rudel, R. G. (1976). Rapid automatized naming (RAN) – Dyslexia differentiated from other learning-disabilities. *Neuropsychologia*, 14 (4), 471-479.
Doman, R. J., Spitz, E. B., Zucman, E., Delacato, C. H. et al. (1960). Children with severe brain injuries. Neurological organization in terms of mobility. *The Journal of the American Medical Association*, *174*, 257–262.
Dreyfus, H. L., & Dreyfus, S. (1990). *Mind over machine: The power of human intuition and expertise in the era of the computer*. New York: Free Press.
Duane, D. D., & Gray, D. B. (Eds.). (1991). *The reading brain: the biological basis of dyslexia*. Parkton, MD: York Press.
Eden, G. F., & Zeffiro, T. A. (1998). Neural systems affected in developmental dyslexia revealed by functional neuroimaging. *Neuron*, *21*, 279–282.

Elliott, C. D. (1990). Definition and identification of specific learning difficulties. In P. D. Pumfrey & C. D. Elliot (Eds.), *Children's difficulties in reading, spelling and writing*. Basingstoke: Falmer Press.

Elliott, J. G., & Gibbs, S. (2008). Does dyslexia exist? *Journal of Philosophy of Education, 42*(3–4), 475–491.

Ellis, A. W. (1993). *Reading, writing and dyslexia: A cognitive analysis* (2nd ed.). London: Lawrence Erlbaum.

Fawcett, A. J., & Nicolson, R. I. (1995). The dyslexia early screening test. *The Irish Journal of Psychology, 16*(3), 248–259.

Fawcett, A. J., & Nicolson, R. I. (1994). Speed of processing, motor skill, automaticity and dyslexia. In A. J. Fawcett & R. I. Nicolson (Eds.), *Dyslexia in children. Multidisciplinary perspectives*. (pp. 157–190). New York, NY: Harwester Wheatsheaf.

Feagens, L. V., Short, E. J., & Meltzer, L. J. (Eds.). (1991). *Subtypes of learning disabilities. Theoretical Perspectives and research*. Hillsdale, NJ: Lawrence Erlbaum Associates.

Filipek, P. A. (1999). Neuroimaging in the developmental disorders: The state of the science. *Journal of Child Psychology and Psychiatry and Allied disciplines, 40*(1), 113–128.

Fisher, S. E., & DeFries, J. C. (2002). Developmental dyslexia: Genetic dissection of a complex cognitive trait. *Neuroscience, 3*, 767–780.

Flanagan, O. (1991). *The science of the mind* (2nd ed.). Cambridge, MA: MIT Press.

Fletcher, J. M. (1992). The validity of distinguishing children with language and learning disabilities according to discrepancies with IQ: introduction to the special series. *Journal of Learning Disabilities, 25*, 546–548.

Fletcher, J. M., & Morris, R. (1986). Classification of disabled learners: Beyond exclusionary definitions. In S. J. Cicci (Ed.), *Handbook of cognitive, social and neuropsychological aspects of learning disabilities* (Vol. I). Hillsdale, NJ: Lawrence Erlbaum Associates.

Fletcher, J. M., Espy, K. A., Francis, D. J., Davidson, K. C., Rourke, B. P., & Shaywitz, S. E. (1989). Comparisons of cutoff and regression-based definitions of reading disabilities. *Journal of Learning Disabilities, 22*, 334–338.

Fletcher, J. M., Shaywitz, S. E., Shankweiler, D., Katz, L., Liberman, I. Y., Steubing, K. K., Francis, D. J., Fowler, A. F., & Shaywitz, B. A. (1994). Cognitive profiles of reading disability: Comparisons of discrepancy and low achievement definitions. *Journal of Educational Psychology, 86*, 6–23.

Fodor, J. A. (1983). *The modularity of mind: An essay on faculty psychology*. Cambridge, MA: MIT Press.

Føllesdal, D. (1979). Hermeneutics and the hypothetico-deductive method. *Dialectica, 33* (3–4), 319–336.

Fredrickson, N., Frith, U., & Reason, R. (1997). *The phonological assessment battery*. Windsor: NFER-Nelson.

Frith, U. (1997). Brain, mind and behaviour in dyslexia. In C. Hulme & M. J. Snowling (Eds.), *Dyslexia: Biology, cognition and intervention*. London: Whurr Publishers.

Frith, U. (1981). Experimental approaches in developmental dyslexia: an introduction. *Psychological Research, 43*, 97–109.

Frith, U. (1986). A developmental framework for developmental dyslexia. *Annals of dyslexia, 36*, 69–81.

Frith, U. (1997). Brain, mind and behavior in dyslexia. In C. Hulme & M. Snowling (Eds.), *Dyslexia: Biology, cognition and intervention* (pp. 2–19). London: Whurr.

Frith, U., & Blakemore, S.-J. (2005). *The learning brain: Lessons for education*. Oxford: Blackwell Publishing.

Gadamer, H.-G. (1960). *Wahrheit und Methode. Grundzüge einer philosophischen Hermeneutik*. Tübingen: Suhrkamp.

Gaffney, J. S., & Anderson, R. C. (2000). Trends in reading research in the United States: Changing intellectual currents over three decades. In M. L. Kamil, P. B. Mosenthall, P. D. Pearson, & R. Barr (Eds.), *Handbook of reading research* (Vol. 3, pp. 53–74). Mahwah, NJ: Erlbaum.

REFERENCES

Galaburda, A. M. (1991). Anatomy of dyslexia: argument against phrenology. In D. D. Duane & D. B. Gray (Eds), *The reading brain: The biological basis of dyslexia*. Parkton, MD: York Press.

Galaburda, A., & Livingstone, M. (1993). Evidence for a magnocellular defect in developmental dyslexia. *Annals of the New York Academy of Sciences, 682*, 70–82.

Gardner, H. (1985). *The mind's new science. A history of the cognitive revolution*. New York: Basic Books.

Geertz, C. (1973). *Local knowledge*. New York, NY: Basic Books.

Geswind, N., & Galaburda, A. M. (1985). Cerebral lateralization. Biological mechanisms, associations and pathology: II. A hypotesis and a program for research. *Archives of Neurology, 42*, 521–552.

Geschwind, N., & Galaburda, A. (1987). *Cerebral lateralization*. Cambridge, MA: MIT.

Gillingham, A., & Stillman, B. E. (1969). *Remedial training for children with specific disability in reading. Spelling and penmanship*. Cambridge, MA: Educators' Publishing Service.

Gjessing, H. J. (1977). *Lese- og skrivevansker. Dysleksi*. Oslo: Universitetsforlaget.

Gjessing, H. J., Nygaard, H. D. og Solheim, R. (1988): *Bergensprosjektet. Utviklingsforløp og læringsproblemer hos elever i grunnskolen III. Studier av barn med dysleksi og andre lærevansker*. Oslo: Universitetsforlaget.

Gombert, J. E. (1992). *Metalinguistic development*. London: Harvester-Whearsheaf.

Goodman, K. (1996). *On reading*. NH: Heinemann.

Goodman, K. S. (1967). Reading: A psycholinguistic guessing game. *Journal of the Reading Specialist, 4*, 126–135.

Goodman, Y. M., & Goodman, K. S. (1994). To err is human: Learning about language processes by analyzing miscues. In R. B. Ruddell, M. R. Ruddell, & H. Singer (Eds.), *Theoretical models and processes of reading*. Newark, DE: IRA.

Goswami, U., & Bryant, P. (1990). *Phonological skills and learning to read*. Hove: Erlbaum.

Gough, P. B., & Tunmer, W. E. (1986). Decoding, reading, and reading disability. *Remedial and Special Education, 7*, 6–10.

Gough, P. B., Ehri, L. C., Treiman, T. (Eds). (1992). *Reading acquisition*. Hillsdale, NJ: Lawrence Erlbaum Associates.

Goulandris, N. (2003). *Dyslexia in different languages: Cross-linguistic comparisons*. London: Whurr Publishers.

Grigorenko, E. L. (2001). Developmental dyslexia: An update on genes, brains, and environment. *Journal of Child Psychology and Psychiatry, 42*, 91–125.

Guthrie, J. T., Wigfield, A., & Perencevich, K. C. (Eds.) (2004). *Motivating reading comprehension: Concept-oriented reading instruction*. Mahwah, NJ: Erlbaum.

Hallgren, B. (1950). Specific dyslexia (congenital word-blindness): A clinical and genetic study. *Acta Psychiatrica et Neurologica, 65* (Suppl.), 1–287.

Harris, T., & Hodges, R. (1985). *The literacy dictionary*. Newark, DE: International Reading Association.

Hatcher, P. J., Hulme, C., & Ellis, A. W. (1994). Ameliorating early reading failure by integrating the teaching of reading and phonological skills: The phonological linkage hypothesis. *Child Development, 65*, 41–57.

Heider, E. R. (1972) Universals in color naming and memory. *Journal of Experimental Psychology, 93*, 10–20.

Helland, T., & Rommetveit, K. (2006). Current dyslexia research seen in the light of Imre Lakatos' philosophy of research programmes. In C. B. Hayes (Ed.), *Dyslexian children: New research* (pp. 103–122). New York: Nova Science Publishers.

Hempel, C. G. (1966). *Philosophy of natural science*. Englewood Cliffs, NJ: Prentice-Hall.

Hergenhahn, B. R. (1986). *An introduction to the history of psychology*. Pacific Grove: Brooks/Cole Publishing Company.

Herman, K. (1959). Reading *disability*. Copenhagen: Munksgaard.

Hinshelwood, J. (1917). *Congenital word blindness*. London: H.K. Lewis.

Hoffman, J. V. (1987). Rethinking the role of oral reading in basal instruction. *Elementary School Journal, 87*, 367–373.

Huey, E. B. (1908). *The psychology and pedagogy of reading. With a review of the history of reading and writing and of methods, texts, and hygiene in reading.* New York: The Macmillan Company.

Hyatt, A. V. (1943). *The place of oral reading in the school program: Its history and development from 1880–1941.* New York: Teachers College, Columbia University.

Hynd, G. W., & Semrud-Clikeman, M. (1989). Dyslexia and brain morphology. *Psychological Bulletin, 106*, 447–482.

Johnson, D. J. (1994) Measurement of listening and speaking. In G. R. Lyon (Ed.), *Frames of reference for the assessment of learning disabilities: New views on measurement issues.* Baltimore, MD: Paul H. Brookes.

Johnston, S. (2006). The fluency assessment system: Improving oral reading fluency with technology. In T. Rasinski, C. Blachowicz, & K. Lems (Eds.), *Fluency instruction* (pp. 123–140). New York: Guilford Press.

Kavale, K. A., & Forness, S. R. (1992). History, definition and diagnosis. In N. N. Singh & I. L. Beale (Eds.), *Learning disabilities: Nature, theory and treatment.* New York, NY: Springer Verlag.

Knapp, T. (1986). The emergence of cognitive psychology in the latter half of the twentieth century. In T. J. Knapp & L. C. Robertson (Eds.), *Approaches to cognition: Contrasts and controversies* (pp. 13–35). Hillsdale, NJ: Erlbaum.

Kreitler, H., & Kreitler, S. (1976). *Cognitive orientation and behavior.* New York: Springer Verlag.

Kuhn, T. S. (1970). *The structure of scientific revolutions* (2nd ed.). Chicago: University of Chicago Press.

LaBerge, D., & Samuels, S. A. (1974). Toward a theory of automatic information processing in reading. *Cognitive Psychology, 6*, 293–323.

Leahey, T.H. (2001). *A history of modern psychology.* Englewood Cliffs, NJ: Prentice Hall.

Leimar, U. (1974). *Läsning på talets grund.* Lund: Liber Läromedel.

Liberman, A. M. (1997). How theories of speech affect research in reading and writing. In B. A. Blachrnan (Ed.), *Foundations of reading acquisition and dyslexia: Implications for early intervention* (pp. 3–19). Mahwah, NJ: Erlbaurn.

Liberman, I. Y. (1973). Desegmentation of the spoken word and reading acquisition. *Bulletin of the Orton Society, 23*, 65–77.

Liberman, I. Y., & Shankweiler, D. (1979). Speech, the alphabet and teaching to read. In L. B. Resnick & P. A. Weaver (Eds.), *Theory and practice in early reading* (Vol. 2, pp. 109–132). Hillsdale, NJ: Erlbaum.

Liberman, I. Y., Shankweiler, D., & Liberman, A. M. (1989). The alphabetic principle and learning to read. In D. Shankweiler& I. Y. Liberman (Eds.). *Phonology and reading disability. Solving the reading puzzle.* Ann Arbor, MI: The University of Michigan Press.

Lundberg, I., Olofsson, Å., & Wall, S. (1980). Reading and spelling skills in the first school years predicted from phoneme awareness skills in kindergarten. *Scandinavian Journal of Psychology, 21*, 159–173.

Lundberg, I., Frost, J., & Petersen, O. (1988). Effects of an extensive program for stimulating phonological awareness in preschool children. *Reading Research Quarterly, 23*, 263–284.

Lyon, G. R. (1995). Toward a definition of dyslexia. *Annals of Dyslexia, 45*, 3–27.

Lyons, J. (1977). *Semantics* (Vol. I). Cambridge, UK: Cambridge University Press.

Lyytinen, H. (Ed.). (1995). *Comorbidity and developmental neurocognitive disorders.* Hillsdale, NJ: Lawrence Erlbaum.

Lyytinen, H. (Ed.). (2002). *The neuropsychology of developmental dyslexia: A special issue of developmental neuropsychology.* Hillsdale, NJ: Lawrence Erlbaum Associates.

Lyytinen, H., Erskine, J., Aro, M., & Richardson, U. (2007). Reading and reading disorders. In E. Hoff (Ed.), *Blackwell handbook of language development* (pp. 454–474). Blackwell.

REFERENCES

Marshall, J. C., & Newcombe, F. (1973). Patterns of paralexia: A psycholinguistic approach. *Journal of Psycholinguistic Research, 2*, 175–199.

Matejcek, Z. (1968). Report of research group on developmental dyslexia and world literacy. *Bulletin of the Orton Society, 18*, 21–22.

Mattis, S., French, J. H., & Rapin, I. (1975). Dyslexia in children and young-adults – 3 independent neuropsychological syndromes. *Developmental Medicine and Child Neurology, 17*(2), 150–163.

McClelland, J. L., & Rumelhart, D. E. (1981). An interactive activation model of context effects in letter perception: Part 1. An account of basic findings. *Psychological Review, 88*, 375–407.

McClelland, J. L., Rumelhart, D. E., & The PDP Research Group. (1986). *Parallel distributed processing: Explorations in the microstructure of cognition.* Vol 2: *Psychological and biological models* (Chapter 18). Cambridge MA: MIT Press.

McDade, J. E. (1937). A hypothesis for non-oral reading: Argument, experiment, and results. *Journal of Educational Research, 30*, 489–503.

Miles, E. (1995). Can there be a single definition of dyslexia? *Dyslexia, 1*, 37–45.

Miles, E. (1998). *The Bangor dyslexia teaching system.* London: Whurr.

Miles, T. R. (1993). *Dyslexia: The pattern of difficulties.* London: Whurr.

Miles, T. R. (1994). A proposed taxonomy and some consequences. In A. J. Fawcett & R. I. Nicolson (Eds.), *Dyslexia in children. Multidisciplinary perspectives.* New York, NY: Harwester Wheatsheaf.

Miles, T. R. (1997). *The Bangor dyslexia test.* Wisbech, Cambridge: Learning Development Aids.

Miles, T. R., & Miles, E. (2001). *Dyslexia: A hundred years on.* Bristol, PA: Open University Press.

Miller, J., & Schwanenflugel, R. J. (2008). A longitudinal study of the development of reading prosody as a dimension of oral reading fluency in early elementary school children. *Reading Research Quarterly, 3*(4), 336–354.

Moats, L. (1994). Assessment of spelling in learning disabilities research. In G. R. Lyon (Ed.), *Frames of reference for the assessment of learning disabilities: New views on assessment issues.* Baltimore, MD: Paul H. Brookes Publishing.

Moats, L., & Lyon, G. R. (1993). Learning disabilities in the United States: Advocacy, science and the future of the field. *Journal of Learning Disabilities, 26*, 282–294.

Morais, J., Cary, L., Alegria, J., & Bertelson, P. (1979). Does awareness of speech as a sequence of phonemes arise spontaneously. *Cognition, 7*, 323–331.

Morton, J. (1968). *Grammar and computation in language behavior.* Progress Report No. 6, Center for Research in Language and Language Behavior, May 1968. Ann Arbor, MI: University of Michigan.

Morton, J. (1979). Facilitation in word recognition: Experiments causing change in the logogen model. In P. A. Kolers, M. Wrolstad, & H. Bouma (Eds.), *Processing of visible language* (Vol. 1, pp. 259–228). New York: Plenum Press.

Morton, J., & Frith, U. (1994). Causal modeling: A structural approach to developmental psychopathology. In I. D. Cicchetti & D. J. Cohen (Eds.), *Manual for developmental psychopathology* (Vol. I., pp. 357–390). New York, NY.

Myklebust, H. R., & Johnson, D. (1962). Dyslexia in children. *Exceptional Children, 29*(1), 14–25.

National Reading Panel. (2000). *Teaching children to read: An evidence-based assessment of the scientific research literature on reading and its implications for reading instruction.* Washington, DC: National Institute for Child Health and Human Development.

Neisser, U. (1976). *Cognition and reality.* San Francisco, CA: W. H. Freeman.

Nicolson, R. I., & Fawcett, A. J. (1990). Automaticity: A new framework for dyslexia research? *Cognition, 35*(2), 159–182.

Nicolson, R. I., & Fawcett, A. J. (1995). Dyslexia is more than a phonological disability. *Dyslexia, 1*, 19–36.

Nicolson, R., & Fawcett, A. (1997). Development of objective procedures for screening and assessment of dyslexic students in higher education. *Journal of Research in Reading, 20*(1), 77–83.

Nicolson, R. I., & Fawcett, A. J. (2010). *Dyslexia, learning and the brain.* Cambridge, MA: MIT Press.

Olson, R., Forsberg, H., Wise, B., & Rack, J. (1994). Measurement of word recognition, orthographic and phonological skills. In G. R. Lyon (Ed.), *Frames of reference for the assessment of learning disabilities: New views on measurement issues* (pp. 243–277). Baltimore, MD: Paul H. Brookes Publishing.

Olson, R. K., Wise, B., Conners, F., Rack, J., & Fulker, D. (1989). Specific deficits in component reading and language skills: genetic and environmental influences. *Journal of Learning Disabilities, 22,* 339–348.

Olson, R. K., Wise, B., Johnson, M. C., & Ring, J. (1997). The etiology and remediation of phonologically based word recognition and spelling disabilities: Are phonological deficits the whole story? In B. A. Blachman (Ed.), *Foundations of reading acquisition and dyslexia: Implications for early intervention* (pp. 409–430). Mahwah, NJ: Erlbaum.

Omaggio, M. A. (1993). *Teaching language in context.* Boston: Heinle & Heinle.

Orton, S. T. (1925). Word-blindness in school children. *Archives of Neurology and Psychiatry, 14,* 581–615.

Orton, S. T. (1937). *Reading, writing and the speech problems in children and selected papers.* Austin, TX: pro-Ed.

Passmore, J. (1985). *Recent philosophers.* London: Duckworth.

Pennington, B. F. (1999). Toward an integrated understanding of dyslexia: Genetic, neurological and cognitive mechanisms. *Development and Psychopathology, 3,* 329–654.

Perfetti, C. (1985). *Reading ability.* New York: Oxford University Press.

Piaget, J. (1966). *Psychology of intelligence.* Totowa, NJ: Littlefield, Adams.

Pikulski, J. J., & Chard, D. J. (2005). Fluency: Bridge between decoding and reading comprehension. *The Reading Teacher, 58*(6), 510–519.

Polanyi, M. (1973). *Personal knowledge. Towards a post-critical philosophy.* London: Routledge & Kegan Paul.

Popper, K. (1959). *The logic of scientific discovery.* London: Hutchinson & Co.

Popper, K. (1963). *Conjectures and refutations: The growth of scientific knowledge.* Oxford: Routledge & Kegan Paul.

Popper, K. (1977). The worlds 1, 2 and 3. In K. Popper & J. C. Eccles (Eds.), *The self and its brain* (pp. 36–50). New York: Springer Verlag.

Pressley, M. (2006). *Reading instruction that works. The case for balanced teaching.* New York: Guilford Press.

Quine, W. V. (1969). *Ontological relativity and other essays.* New York, NY: Columbia University Press.

Rasinski, T. V. (1990). Effects of repeated reading and listening-while-reading on reading fluency. *Journal of Educational Research, 83,* 147–150.

Rasinski, T. V., & Hoffman, T. V. (2003). Theory and research into practice: Oral reading in the school literacy curriculum. *Reading Research Quarterly, 38,* 510–522.

Rasinski, T. V., Padak, N., Linek, W., & Sturtevant, E. (1994). The effects of fluency development instruction on urban second grader readers. *Journal of Educational Research, 87,* 158–164.

Rayner, K., & Pollatsek, A. (1989). *The psychology of reading.* Englewood Cliffs, NJ: Prentice Hall.

Reber, A. S. (1993). *Implicit learning and tacit knowledge. An essay on the cognitive unconscious.* Oxford, England: Oxford University Press.

Reber, A. S. (1995). *Dictionary of psychology* (2nd ed.). London: Penguin Books.

Riese, W. (1953). *The conception of disease, its history, its versions and its nature.* New York, NY: Wiley.

Rodgers, G. E. (2001). *The history of beginning reading: From teaching by sound to teaching by meaning* (Vols. 1–3). London: 1st Book Library.

Rogers, T. T., & McClelland, J. L. (2004). *Semantic cognition: A parallel distributed processing approach.* Cambridge, MA: MIT Press.

Rohrer, J. H. (1943). An analysis and evaluation of the 'non-oral' method of reading instruction. *Elementary School Journal, 43,* 415–421.

Rosch, E., & Lloyd, B. B. (1978). *Cognition and categorization.* Hillsdale, NJ: Lawrence.

Rourke, B. P. (Ed.). (1985). *Neuropsychology of learning disabilities. Essentials of subtype analysis.* New York, NY: Guilford Press.

Rumelhart, D. E. (1984). The emergence of cognitive phenomena from the subsymbolic processes. In *Proceedings of the Sixth Annual Conference of the Cognitive Science Society* (pp. 59–62). Boulder, CO: Cognitive Science Society.

Rumelhart, D. E. (1994). Toward an interactive model of reading. In R. B. Ruddell, M. R. Ruddell, & H. Singer (Eds.), *Theoretical models and processes of reading* (4th ed., p. 893). Newark: International Reading Association.

Rumelhart, D. E., & McClelland, J. L. (1982). An interactive activation model of context effects in letter perception: Part 2. The contextual enhancement effect and some tests and extensions of the model. *Psychological Review, 89,* 60–94.

Rumelhart, D. E., & McClelland, J. L. (1986). On learning the past tense of English verbs. In J. L. McClelland, D. E. Rumelhart, & The PDP Research Group (Eds.), *Parallel distributed processing: explorations in the microstructure of cognition* (Vol. 2, pp. 216–271). Cambridge, MA: MIT Press.

Rumelhart, D. E., Smolensky, P., McClelland, J. L., & Hinton, G. E. (1986). Schemata and sequential thought processes in PdP models. In J. L. McClelland, D. E. Rumelhart, & The PDP Research Group (Eds.), *Parallel distributed processing: Explorations in the microstructure of cognition* (Vol. 2). Cambridge, MA: MIT Press.

Rutter, M., & Yule, W. (1975). The concept of specific reading retardation. *Journal of Child Psychology and Psychiatry, 16,* 181–197.

Rutter, M., Tizard, J., Yule, W., Graham, P., & Whitmore, K. (1976). Isle-of-Wight studies, 1964–1974. *Psychological Medicine, 6*(2), 313–332.

Sahlins, M. (1976). Colors and cultures. *Semiotica, 16,* 1–22.

Salmon, W. C. (1973). *Logic.* Englewood Cliffs, NJ: Prentice-Hall.

Samuels, S. J., & Farstrup, A. E. (2006). *What research has to say about fluency instruction.* Newark, DE: International Reading Association.

Samuels, S. J., & Kamil, M. (1984). Models of the reading process. In R. D. Pearson (Ed.), *Handbook of reading research* (pp. 185–224). New York: Longman.

Scarborough, H. S. (1990). Very early language deficits in dyslexic children. *Child Development, 61,* 1728–1743.

Schnaitter, R. (1986). A coordination of differences: Behaviorism, mentalism and the foundation of psychology. In T. J. Knapp & L. C. Robertson (Eds.), *Approaches to cognition: Contrasts and controversies* (pp. 291–315). Hillsdale, NJ: Erlbaum.

Seidenberg, M. S., & McClelland, J. L. (1989). A distributed developmental model of word recognition and naming. *Psychological Review, 96,* 523–568.

Seymour, P. H. K. (1986). *Cognitive analysis of dyslexia.* London: Routledge & Kegan Paul.

Seymour, P. H. K. (2005). Early reading development in European orthographies. In M. J. Snowling & C. Hulme (Eds.), *The science of reading: A handbook* (pp. 296–315). Oxford: Blackwell.

Seymour, P. H. K., & Porpodas, C. D. (1980). Lexical and non-lexical processing of spelling in developmental dyslexia. In U. Frith (Ed.), *Cognitive processes in spelling* (pp. 443–473). London: Academic Press.

Shankweiler, D., & Liberman, I. Y. (Eds.). (1989). *Phonology and reading disability. Solving the puzzle.* Ann Arbor, MI: The University of Michigan Press.

Share, D. L., & Stanovich, K. E. (1995) Cognitive processes in early reading development: accommodating individual differences into a mode of acquisition. *Issues in Education: Contributions from Educational Psychology, 1,* 1–57.

Shaywitz, B. A., & Shaywitz, S. E. (1994). Measuring and analysing change. In G. R. Lyon (Ed.), *Frames of reference for the assessment of learning disabilities: New views on measurement issues.* Baltimore, MD: Paul H. Brookes Publishing.

Shaywitz, B. A., Fletcher, J. M., & Shaywitz, S. E. (1995). Defining and classifying learning disabilities and attention-deficit/hyperactivity disorder. *Journal of Child Neurology, 10,* 5057.

Shaywitz, S. E., Escobar, M. D., Shaywitz, B. A., Fletcher, J. M., & Makugh, R. (1992). Evidence that dyslexia may represent the lower tail of a normal distribution of reading ability. *New England Journal of Medicine, 326*, 145–150.

Siegel, L. S. (1989a). IQ is irrelevant to the definition of learning disabilities. *Journal of Learning Disabilities, 22*, 469–478.

Siegel, L. S. (1989b). Why we do not need intelligence scores in the definition and analyses of learning disabilities. *Journal of Learning Disabilities, 22*, 514–518.

Simon, H. A., & Newell, A. (1964). Information processing in computer and man. *American Scientist, 52*, 281–300.

Simos, P. G., Fletcher, J. M., Bergman, E., Breier, J. I., Foorman, B. R., Castillo, E. M., et al. (2002). Dyslexia-specific brain activation profile becomes normal following successful remedial training. *Neurology, 58*(8), 1203–1213.

Skinner, B. F. (1984). Author's response. *The Behavioral and Brain Sciences, 7*, 655–667.

Skinner, B. F. (1986). Why I am not a cognitive psychologist. In T. J. Knapp & L. C. Robertson (Eds.), *Approaches to cognition: Contrasts and controversies* (pp. 79–90). Hillsdale, NJ: Erlbaum.

Skinner, B. F. (1938). *Behavior of organisms*. New York: Appleton-Century-Crofts.

Smith, F. (1971). *Understanding reading: A psycholinguistic analysis of reading and learning to read*. New York: Holt, Rinehart.

Snow, C. E., Burns, S., & Griffin, P. (Eds.). (1998). *Preventing reading difficulties in young children*. Washington, DC: National Academy Press.

Snowling, M. J., Goulandris, N., Bowlby, M., & Howell, P. (1986). Segmentation and speech perception in relation to reading skill: A developmental analysis. *Journal of Experimental Child Psychology, 41*, 489–507.

Stanovich, K. E. (1980). Toward an interactive-compensatory model of individual differences in the development of reading fluency. *Reading Research Quarterly, 16*, 32–71.

Stanovich, K. E. (1991). Word recognition: Changing perspectives. In R. Barr, M. L. Kamil, P. Mosenthal, & P. D. Pearson (Eds.), *Handbook of reading research* (Vol. 2, pp. 418–452). New York: Longman.

Stanovich, K. E. (1992). Response to Christensen. *Reading Research Quarterly, 27*, 279–280.

Stanovich, K. E. (1993). The construct validity of discrepancy definitions of reading disability. In G. R. Lyon, D. Gray, J. Kavanagh, & N. Krasnegor (Eds.), *Better understanding learning disabilities: New views on research and their implications for public policies*. Baltimore, MD: Paul H. Brookes Publishing.

Stanovich, K. E. (1994). Annotation: does dyslexia exist? *Journal of Child Psychology and Psychiatry, 35*(4), 579–595.

Stanovich, K. E., & Siegel, L. S. (1994). Phenotypic performance profile of children with reading disabilities: A regression-based test of the phonological-core variable-difference model. *Journal of Educational Psychology, 86*, 24–53.

Stein, J. (2001). The magnocellular theory of developmental dyslexia. *Dyslexia, 7*, 12–36.

Stein, J., & Fowler, S. (1985). Effect of monocular occlusion on visuomotor perception and reading in dyslexic children. *The Lancet, 2*(8446), 69–73.

Stein, J. & Walsh, V. (1997). To see but not to read; the magnocellular theory of dyslexia. *Trends in Neuroscience, 20*, 147–152.

Stirling, E. G., & Miles, T. R. (1988). Naming ability and oral fluency in dyslexic adolescents. *Annals of Dyslexia, 38*, 50–72.

Studdert-Kennedy, M. (1991). Language development from evolutionary perspective. In N. A. Krasnegor, D. M. Rumbaugh, R. L. Schiefelbusch, & M. Studdert-Kennedy (Eds.), *Biological determinants of language development*. London: Erlbaum.

Tallal, P., Miller, S. L., Jenkins, W. M., & Merzenich, M. M. (1997). The role of temporal processing in developmental language-based learning disorders: Research and clinical implications. In B. A. Blachman (Ed.), *Foundations of reading acquisition and dyslexia: Implications for early intervention* (pp. 49–66). Mahwah, NJ: Erlbaum.

119

REFERENCES

Thomas Aquinas, *Truth* (Trans. Robert W. Mulligan) (Vol. 1: 1–9); James V. McGlynn (vol. 2: 10–20), Robert W. Schmidt (vol. 3: 21–29). Chicago: H. Regnery, 1952–1954; reprint: Indianapolis: Hackett, 1994.

Thomson, M. (1990). *Developmental dyslexia* (3rd ed.) London: Whurr.

Thorne, B. M., & Henley, T. B. (2001). *Connections in the history and systems of psychology.* Boston, MA: Houghton Mifflin Company.

Tønnessen, F. E. (1995). On defining 'dyslexia'. *Scandinavian Journal of Educational Research, 39,* 139–156.

Tønnessen, F. E. (1997a). How can we best define 'dyslexia'? *Dyslexia, 3,* 78–92.

Tønnessen, F. E. (1997b). Testosterone and dyslexia. *Pedriatric Rehabilitation, 1*(1), 51–57.

Tønnessen, F. E. (1997c). Treating dyslexia and teaching reading. *Nordic Journal of Special Education, 3,* 100–106.

Tønnessen, F. E. (1999). Awareness and automaticity in reading. In I. Lundberg, F. E. Tønnessen, & I. Austad (Eds.), *Dyslexia: advances in theory and practice* (pp. 91–99). Dordrecht/Boston/London: Kluwer Academic Publishers.

Tønnessen, F. E. (2011). What are skills? Some fundamental reflections. *L1 – Educational Studies in Language and Literature,* pp. 149–158.

Tønnessen, F. E., Løkken, A., Høien, T., & Lundberg, I. (1993). Dyslexia, left-handedness and immune disorders. *Archives of Neurology, 50,* 411–416.

Torgesen, K., Wagner, R. K., & Rashotte, C. A. (1997). Prevention and remediation of severe reading disabilities: Keeping the end in mind. *Scientific Studies of Reading, 1,* 217–234.

Uppstad, P. H. (2005). *Language and literacy. Some fundamental issues in research on reading and writing.* Lund: Department of Linguistics.

Vellutino, F. R. (1979). *Dyslexia: Theory and research.* Cambridge, MA: MIT Press.

Vellutino, F. R., Scanlon, D. M., & Tanzman, M. S. (1994). Components of reading ability: issues and problems in operationalizing word identification, phonological coding and orthographical coding. In G. R. Lyon (Ed.), *Frames of reference for the assessment of learning disabilities: New views on measurement issues.* Baltimore, MD: Paul H. Brookes Publishing.

Vellutino, F. R., Scanlon, D. M., Sipay, E. R., Small, S. G., Pratt, A., Chen, R. S., & Denckla, M. B. (1996). Cognitive profiles of difficult to remediate and readily remediated poor readers: Early intervention as a vehicle for distinguishing between cognitive and experiential deficits as basic causes of specific reading disability. *Journal of Educational Psychology, 88,* 601–638.

Vellutino, F. R., Scanlon, D. M., & Lyon, G. R. (2000). Differentiating between difficult-to-remediate and readily remediated poor readers: More evidence against the IQ–achievement discrepancy definition of reading disability. *Journal of Learning Disabilities, 33,* 223–238.

Vellutino, F. R., Fletcher, J. M., Snowling, M. J., & Scanlon, D. M. (2004). Specific reading disability (dyslexia): what have we learned in the past four decades? *Journal of Child Psychology and Psychiatry, 45*(1), 2–40.

Vernon, M. D. (1957). *Backwardness in reading: A study of its nature and origin.* University Press.

von Eckardt, B. (1993). *What is cognitive science?* Cambridge, MA: MIT Press.

von Engelhardt, D., & Schipperges, H. (1980). *Die inneren Verbindung zwischen Philosophie und Medizin im 20. Jahrhundert.* Darmstadt: Wissenschaftliche Buchgesellschaft.

von Wright, G. H. (1971). *Explanation and understanding.* London: Routledge & Kegan Paul.

Wagner, R. K., & Torgesen, J. J. (1987). The nature of phonological processing, and its causal role in the acquisition of reading skills. *Psychological Bulletin, 101,* 192–212.

Watson, J. B. (1930). *Behaviorism* (2nd ed.). New York: Norton.

Wheeler, T., & Watkins, E. J. (1979) A review of symptomatology. *Dyslexia Review, 2,* 12–16.

Wimmer, H., Landerl, K., & Schneider, W. (1994). The role of rhyme awareness in learning to read a regular orthography. *British Journal of Developmental Psychology, 12,* 469–484.

Wise, B. W., Olson, R. K., & Ring, J. (1997). Teaching phonological awareness with and without the computer. In C. Hulme & M. Snowling (Eds.), *Dyslexia: Biology, cognition and intervention* (pp. 254–275). London: Whurr.

Wittgenstein, L. (1922/1961). *Tractatus logico-philosophicus* (Transl. D. F. Pears & B. F. McGuinness). London: Routledge and Kegan Paul.

Wittgenstein, L. (1953/2005). *Philosophische Untersuchungen* (Transl. G. E. M. Anscombe, P. S. M. Hacker, & J. Schulte) (4th ed.). London: Blackwell Publishing.

Wolf , M. (1979). *The relationship of disorders of word-finding and reading in children and aphasics.* Unpublished doctoral dissertation. Harvard University.

Wolf, M. (1984). Naming, reading, and the dyslexias – A longitudinal overview. *Annals of Dyslexia, 34,* 87–115.

Wolf, M., & Bowers, P. (1999). The "Double-Deficit Hypothesis" for the developmental dyslexia. *Journal of Educational Psychology, 91,* 1–24.

Wolf, M., & Katzir-Cohen, T. (2001). Reading fluency and its intervention. *Scientific Studies of Reading, 5*(3), 211–229.

Wood, F., Felton, R., Flowers, L., & Naylor, C. (1991). Neurobehavioral definition of dyslexia. In D. D. Duane & D. B. Gray (Eds.), *The reading brain: The biological basis of dyslexia.* Parkton, MD: York Press.

Yap, R., & van der Leij, A. (1993a). Rate of elementary symbol processing in dyslexics. In S. F. Wright & R. Groner (Eds.), *Facets of dyslexia and its remediation* (pp. 337–349). Amsterdam: Elsevier Science Publishers.

Yap, R., & van der Leij, A. (1993b). Word processing in dyslexics: An automatic decoding deficit? *Reading and Writing: An Interdisciplinary Journal, 5,* 261–279.

Yap, R., & van der Leij, A. (1994). Testing the automatization deficit hypothesis of dyslexia via a dual-task paradigm. *Journal of Learning Disabilities, 27,* 660–665.

Zadeh, L. A. (1975). Fuzzy logic and approximate reasoning. *Synthese, 30,* 407–428.

SUBJECT INDEX

NAME INDEX